Murder & Crime &

S E R I E S

DOVER

When it's dark in Dover
It's dark the whole world over.
(Old Saying)

Unlimited power is apt to corrupt the minds of those who possess it.
(Speech at the House of Lords, 1770)

... as unattractive morally as crime may be, we must appreciate that there is genuine experiential creativity in it as well. We should then be able to see what are, for the subject, the authentic attractions of crime and we should be able to explain variations in criminality beyond what can be accounted for by background factors.
(J. Katz, *Moral and Sensual Attractions in Doing Evil*, Basic Books, 1988)

Murder & Crime
SERIES

DOVER

JANET CAMERON

The History Press

Photos by Philip Howdle unless otherwise stated.

First published 2006
Reprinted 2007

Reprinted in 2009 by
The History Press
The Mill, Brimscombe Port,
Stroud, Gloucestershire, GL5 2QG
www.thehistorypress.co.uk

British Library Cataloguing in Publication Data.
A catalogue record for this book is available from the British Library.

ISBN 978 07524 3987 5

Typesetting and origination by
Tempus Publishing Limited.
Printed in Great Britain.

Contents

Acknowledgements

Grateful thanks to the following for sharing their valuable expertise, advice and research with me for the benefit of this book:

Dover District Council
The Prince of Wales Sea Training School, Dover
The Port of Dover;
Richard Clark, author of *Capital Punishment UK* (www.richard.clark32.btinternet.co.uk)
'Dover Pages' Website with special thanks for 'Between a Rock and a Hard Place' page 51 and
 'I Won't Pay Nothing' page 65.
www.dover-kent.co.uk
Buckland Hospital
Dover, Margate and Birchington Libraries
June and John English
Peter E. Blanche
Jonathan Marsh for a wealth of information about Dover's prisons and pubs
Dorothy Bayliss and Robert Whitewood of Dover Museum

My editors, Katherine Burton, Ed Palmer and Cate Ludlow for their support and advice.

Introduction

This book focuses primarily on Dover and its immediate surrounding villages, but there will be some references to other places in east Kent. Due to the nature of some of the crimes, particularly smuggling and wrecking, there was continual movement and commercial interaction between Dover and its neighbouring villages and towns. For example, smuggling gangs from Aldington and Hawkhurst also terrorised Dover and nearby Deal. The coastal town of Deal's wrecking activities would not have proven nearly as profitable but for the ships foundering on the perilous Goodwin Sands *en route* to Dover's famous port. Contraband from the other Cinque Ports frequently found its way to Dover's merchants, and a soldiers' mutiny in Folkestone sparked off a copycat uprising in Dover.

Some chapters cover personal and specific moments in Dover's history, contrasting the so-called crimes of the historical past with those of the more recent past, and revealing their all-too-frequently terrible consequences. The persecution of witches, the press gangs, domestic murder and violence, street crime, fraud, petty thievery, desertion and immorality are just a few of the crimes covered in this book. Some of the 'crimes' committed then would not be regarded as crimes today – and vice versa. In many cases in Dover's dark past, crime was the only way for poor communities to feed their children.

I hope this book will help you to enjoy Dover's colourful heritage – its finest moments and especially its darkest hours. They helped make the town what it is today, a special place as diverse as the people who formerly inhabited and created it.

A Brief Outline of Dover's History

> 'Drive towards Dover, friend, where thou shalt meet welcome.'
> *(King Lear*, William Shakespeare)

The important seaport of Dover lies fifteen miles south-east of Canterbury on the east coast of Kent. Its name is derived from the Dour, a stream running through a valley between Walmer and Sandgate, and comes from the Celtic word *dubräs*, meaning 'the waters'. The discovery of a Bronze-Age cargo boat in 1992 dating from 1550 BC indicates that Dover has been a port for at least 3,500 years. To the best of our knowledge, this is the most ancient sea-going vessel ever discovered. It is on display in Dover Museum.

Dover was always a busy seaport due to its close proximity to the French coast, just twenty-one miles away and easily seen from the towering chalk cliffs on a clear day. When the Romans first tried to invade Dover, they had to withdraw due to the barbaric warriors who hurled stones at them from the cliff tops. Eventually, in AD 43, they succeeded in landing at Deal. The seaport at Dover was developed by the Romans from the natural harbour created by the Dour,

Opposite: *Dover Castle from Castle Street.*

Right: *Opposite view: Castle Street from Dover Castle.*

and became their foremost naval base after Julius Caesar invaded in 55 BC with 6,000 men and eighty boats. The Romans also built the lighthouse, the Eastern Pharos, located within the castle grounds although it predates the castle. Adjacent is the Saxon church, St Mary-in-Castro (AD 1000), to the south of which a graveyard has offered evidence of many Saxon burials. A second (western) Pharos was built by the Romans on Western Heights although all that remains today is the Bredenstone, a pile of masonry.

After the Romans withdrew in 449, the Saxons arrived at Pegwell Bay and took over. The Saxon name for Dover was Dofras. In 1066, in retaliation for Saxon resistance, the Normans burnt down much of Dover, though William the Conqueror later rebuilt it.

To protect the harbour from invasion, work on Dover Castle began in 1180 and the structure remained a military fortress until the 1960s. The Western Docks, as the original harbour is known, date from the early 1500s (Henry VIII's reign). Elizabeth I continued the work in 1595, imposing a tax on all shipping to pay for it. Eventually Dover became the founder member of the Confederation of Cinque Ports (pronounced sink), which was instigated by Edward I. The Cinque Ports were first mentioned in a royal charter of 1155. As there was no Navy at this time, the ports agreed to supply ships for the Crown when needed in return for certain privileges.

'The Pharos', Dover's Roman Lighthouse. Originally, it was eighty feet high.

They abused these privileges by practising open piracy around the Kent and Sussex coast, and there was no one to stop them from wrecking and plundering other vessels. They were also permitted to mete out 'justice' through their own courts.

The five founding towns of the Cinque Ports were Dover, Sandwich, Hythe, Romney and Hastings and later, Rye and Winchelsea were added to Hastings. The role of the Cinque Ports was at its height in the thirteenth century, and, although the King was served, they continued to deal in piracy, robbery and pillage. Gradually decline set in during the fourteenth century as many harbours silted up; when Dover's original harbour silted up in the 1800s, a replacement had to be built out in the English Channel and, eventually, the old harbour disappeared beneath the town. Around this time, Dover's close neighbour, Deal, had risen in the ranks, becoming a much-feared vortex of pirates, smugglers and cut-throats.

The title of Lord Warden of the Cinque Ports was held by Wellington, and after his death in 1852, it was passed on to MP W.H. Smith. The late HM Queen Elizabeth, the Queen Mother, was a recent Lord Warden: she followed on from Sir Robert Menzies, former Prime Minister of Australia, in 1978.

During the World Wars, a great deal of Dover was destroyed, and the seaport town and adjacent coastline became known as Hellfire Corner, due to the air raids and fire from long-range guns on the French coast. However, two major Second World War operations were conducted from Dover Castle's secret wartime tunnels by Vice Admiral Bertram Home Ramsey (1883-1945). The first was Operation Dynamo in May 1940, when the Germans breached the Maginot Line and were closing on British troops trapped at Dunkirk. The enormous success of Vice Admiral Ramsey's command, and the courage of the heroic men who set out in a flotilla of fishing boats to rescue the desperate, stranded troops, was immortalised on 31 May 1940, in the *Daily Express's* main headline: 'TENS OF THOUSANDS SAFELY HOME ALREADY'. The second operation was the Normandy invasion in 1944, when Vice Admiral Ramsey conducted affairs as Allied Naval Commander-in-Chief.

The secret wartime tunnels were originally excavated in 1797 by miners who had been instructed by the Royal Engineers to provide secure, underground barracks for soldiers. During the Napoleonic Wars, they were occupied by around 2,000 men.

Despite the cruel bombardment Dover received during wartime, precious relics from the past remain: an Elizabethan mansion, Maison Dieu House, located next to Dover Town Hall, dates from 1665 and was the residence of the Agent Victualler (a Navy official who controlled the supplying of the Channel Fleet) until the Battle of Waterloo. It then became a private residence, and is now the property of the Dover Corporation and used as a library. Castle Street, from which there is a fine view of the castle, is one of Dover's oldest surviving areas. From 1903, the Navy's Channel fleet ceased to operate in Dover.

Stone tablet from 1827, with the spelling DOVOR.

Aerial view of the harbour (by kind permission of the Port of Dover).

Today, despite the changes, Dover is still what it has always been within recorded memory, an important and historical British port with its famous white cliffs dominating the most fascinating stretch of coastline in the world.

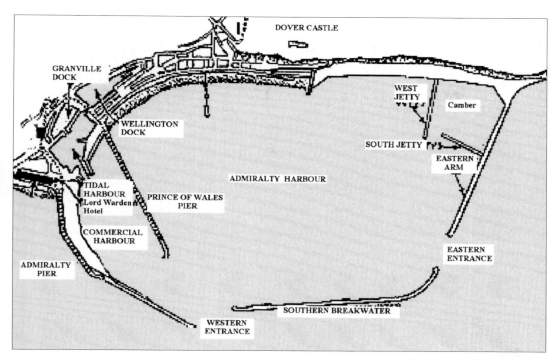

Aerial diagram of the harbour (by kind permission of The Prince of Wales Sea Training School).

Western Arm Docks from Military Hill, 1963, by Nicholas Green (by kind permission of The Prince of Wales Sea Training School).

Place Names

Below are some of the place names of Dover, excluding the town centre, together with their origins. (Names which are self-explanatory are not included.)

Aycliffe: High cliff.

Barton: Barley Farm.

Braddon: 'Brad' = broad.

Buckland and Buckland Valley: land granted by deed or charter.

Burgoyne Heights: From 'Burgoyne Fort'. The English General John Burgoyne surrendered to America at Saratoga in 1877 during the War of Independence.

Crabble: Crab Hole. There may have been a creek nearby where crabs were caught.

Charlton: Peasants' farmstead. (Charl: churls or peasants).

Kearsney: Place where cress grows.

Maxton: Maca's stone. 'Maca' was a landowner, *OE* 'Macan'.

St Radigunds: From St Radigund's Abbey. St Radigund (*c.* AD 520-587) was the daughter of a murdered Thuringian (central German) King, captured by the brutal, dissolute Frankish King, Clothaire, and made his Queen. She escaped and lived as a nun.

Whitfield: Whit means white or chalky = chalky open ground.

Temple Ewell: Temple = Knights Templars. Ewell = source of a stream.

Surrounding Villages

Barfreston: Beornfriðs' farmstead.

Coldred: Clearing where charcoal is burnt.

I

WITCHCRAFT

It is widely believed that the term witch is derived from the Old English word *witan*, meaning 'wise person'. An alternative possibility is *Wicca* (masculine) and *Wicce* (feminine), another pair of Old English terms related to the verb *wiccian*, meaning to practise magic arts. Although long ago, both genders were known as witches, later the term was applied only to women, while 'male witches' would be described as sorcerers, warlocks or wizards.

The first legislation against witchcraft came into force in the mid-seventh century as part of a mission by Theodore, Archbishop of Canterbury to suppress Pagan practices. By the twelfth century, Christians had begun to associate witchcraft with the rejection of God, or even with demonic possession. Towards the end of the century, the dreaded Inquisition, an ecclesiastical court founded by Pope Gregory IX around 1232, had taken hold in northern Italy and southern France. Both the Papal Inquisition and the Spanish Inquisition, established in 1478 to deal with religious heretics, later included Protestants as targets for persecution.

During the dark times of the fifteenth century, witch-hunts became a serious business, and the mass persecution of women accused of witchcraft became rife. Whatever religion was in power at the time, first Catholic, then Protestant, witches were defined as heretics who made a pact with the Devil to obtain power. Under Elizabeth I and James I around 1,000 people were burned or hanged as witches, the last official execution taking place in 1685. It is claimed 30,000 to 50,000 witches were executed between the fifteenth and the nineteenth centuries by a number of grisly methods: burning, strangulation, beheading or hanging. Most of those persecuted were women, but around twenty per cent were men. Almost all of their confessions were extracted by torture.

Witches, it is claimed, appealed for the intervention of evil spirits, performing diabolical rites on the Witches' Sabbath, which parodied the Mass and the practices of the Orthodox Christian Church. They repudiated Jesus and the sacraments in their pursuit of the Prince of Darkness, who rewarded them with supernatural powers.

Dover's Witches

The first recorded witch trial in Dover took place in 1559, when Clement Baker and his wife appeared before the town's mayor, Thomas Colley, and his councillors. Their crime: 'an evil demeanour and behaviour'. The couple were dealt with lightly, for this period in history, and were merely banished for a year and a day from the town of Dover.

Some time later, an elderly woman was not dealt with so leniently. In Coldred, a small village on the outskirts of Dover, the village pond was regularly used for 'swimming' during witch trials, a means of establishing guilt by whether the accused floated or sank. It is recorded that in the 1640s an elderly woman, Nell Garlinge, was tightly bound, her thumbs and toes being tied crosswise, and then hurled into the water. Nell drowned, and was pronounced innocent! The village pond where Nell and other poor women met their fate still exists, although thankfully the only swimming that takes place there today is by the ducks. Nell's tragic story appears on Coldred's historic notice board.

This practice of 'swimming' to catch witches was a no-win situation for many women, who may only have offended a malicious neighbour, or been branded a 'scold' by their husband. If a woman sank and drowned, her innocence was proven as she was hauled out, dead, by a rope around her waist. Many, like Nell Garlinge, did drown, so that ironically their names were cleared in death. However, if a woman floated and was deemed guilty, she would be brought to trial to be hanged or burned at the stake. It is claimed twenty-five per cent of witchcraft claims were made by children informing on their relatives. It can be imagined how terrified mothers must have been of punishing their children too harshly.

Pricking was a means of identifying witches, because people believed that witches bore the mark of the devil on their body and that this area was impervious to pain. To this end, no part of the body was considered sacred, and the accused had to endure being stripped naked and brutally exposed to pain and humiliation.

Witches were also burned at the stake and hanged. The most usual method for burning witches was to tie the condemned woman to the stake and surround her with faggots so she died hidden from sight by a wall of flames. Death may have come from shock or from burned

Coldred village pond, where Nell Garlinge drowned.

lungs as she inhaled the smoke. One witch was hanged in neighbouring Cinque Port, Sandwich, in 1630.

In 1736, the law against witchcraft was repealed, although the witch-hunts continued. The last recorded witch to be hanged in England was Alice Molland in 1686.

Protection Against Witches

During the sixteenth and seventeenth centuries, wines and beers were drawn from barrels into stone or leather bottles which were made in the Netherlands and stamped with an image of Cardinal Robert Bellarmine (1542-1621). The cardinal opposed the Dutch Reformed Church and it is claimed that Protestants took revenge on him by smashing the jugs. However, he was a kindly man, and held in high esteem by the Roman Catholic Church which canonised him in 1930. Cardinal Bellarmine's bottles were used as a protection against witches. First they were filled with certain items, then sealed and buried; this, it was claimed, would defeat the curse of a witch. Mayors of another Cinque Port, Sandwich, still carry, as they have done for centuries, a blackthorn wand intended as protection against the threat of witchcraft.

II

SMUGGLING

Dover and the east coast of Kent were rife with the practice of smuggling, which began in 1300, around the reign of Edward I, when exported wool became liable for customs duty. Prior to this, all trade, both import and export, was free. However, the Hundred Years War proved expensive – and so the tax was hiked up to finance the troops. The export of any wool at all was made illegal in 1614 and smuggling wool had its own term, 'owling', derived from the hooting noises by which smugglers communicated together. Bribery of port officials increased, as, eventually, in 1661, the death sentence was implemented for smuggling wool.

Charles II decided enough was enough in 1671, and so he formed the Board of Customs (although it is claimed there was a Customs House in Dover from around the thirteenth century). During the 1670s, 20,000 packs of wool were sent to Calais each year, and the smugglers armed their ships, sending them out in the dead of night. In retaliation, the revenue used 'sloops', small, single-masted boats with one mainsail, which were sent out to try to catch the smugglers. A group of 'owlers' who preyed on the south coast during the early 1700s were known as the Mayfield Gang, although the main culprit was caught in 1721.

Finally, the French found they could purchase reasonably-priced wool from Ireland and so smuggling this commodity became less attractive and then, in 1784, duty on French wine and tea was reduced. However, this did not stop these determined men from smuggling spirits and tobacco, and this illegal practice became especially lucrative when taxes went up, yet again, to fund another war, this time the Napoleonic Wars of 1797-1815.

It is estimated that during the height of the smugglers' activities, two-thirds of the tea consumed in England had been smuggled.

The Price of Being Caught
The rise in taxes made smuggling a worthwhile way of life – just so long as you didn't get caught! But it was a catch-22 situation: insufficient numbers of customs officers made the practice an acceptable, calculated risk, but, with the prospect of the gibbet looming before them, smugglers had nothing to lose by murdering the revenue men if they were caught.

The Dreaded Gibbet
The gibbet was an upright post with an arm on the top end from which convicted felons were hanged. A bar extended from the back to the neck and the feet. Then an iron ring was placed around the neck: another held the waist and two more were fixed around the ankles.

A smuggler signalling to a lugger lying offshore in 1820 (by kind permission of Dover District Council).

After the hanging, the authorities, in an effort to deter others from emulating the felons, would have the body dipped in tar to render it waterproof, and then the dead felon would be bound in heavy chains so that the corpse would not fall apart as it decomposed - a dire warning against temptation. The unfortunate convict would have first been measured by a blacksmith to determine the length of chain required, and it is said some died of fear before their execution. Another method of displaying the corpse was the gibbet iron. The smell would be appalling and no one dared interfere for fear of reprisal. So the bodies were left, sometimes, it is claimed, for many years.

But encounters between smugglers and revenue men did not always end this way, as many officers were willing to 'look the other way' in return for money or a share of the bounty. Parsons would leave their churches unlocked to allow for the storage of contraband and even magistrates were open to corruption, just as they are today. As for ordinary people – they benefited too, as can be seen from this verse from Rudyard Kipling's poem, *The Smugglers Song*:

Five-and-twenty ponies,
Trotting through the dark,
Brandy for the Parson,
Baccy for the Clerk;
Laces for a lady; letters for a spy,
And watch the wall, my darling, while the Gentlemen go by!

Gangs

In the 1700s, smuggling in Dover was at its zenith, with many men using it as their sole means of livelihood. By 1822, there were sixty-two customs men in Dover. During this time, customs officers were thwarted by the co-operation of the French, whose warehouses in their own ports even supplied goods bound in waterproof packaging. Now smuggling had reached a level of sophistication previously undreamt of.

In the early nineteenth century, English smugglers made themselves useful to Napoleon by carrying information from French spies who plied their profession in England. When required, the smugglers transported the spies safely across the Channel in their galleys, returning with luxuries like silk products and French lace. They also ferried spies from France into England and put them up in 'safe houses' until they were able to make arrangements for dispersal across the country.

Smugglers on the Dover and Folkestone coastline also dealt in golden guineas, (worth twenty-one shillings) selling them in France for around thirty shillings. The guineas were used by Napoleon to pay his armies.

Smuggling was a community business, a way of getting a little of the good life, the wine, the gin, the whisky and tea. Ladies prized the lace, the silk and the gloves. We should, however, be fair on the smugglers. Life was hard, families needed feeding, and smuggling gave work to entire communities, who would help with the landing, unloading and transport of the goods. Prior to despatch or local sale, smugglers' cargo was usually stored in a bar or church with an accommodating publican or vicar. Likewise, the trade provided work for those willing to help by keeping watch. Farm labourers were extremely poor, managing on a subsistence wage (two shillings and sixpence a day during the 1830s).

The Hawkhurst Gang

The Hawkhurst Gang, founded by Arthur Gray in the mid-1700s when they were known as the 'Holkhourst Genge', made use of labourers on low wages who were tempted by the rich pickings to be enjoyed from smuggling. This gang, sometimes 500 strong, terrorised the whole of Kent, including Dover, although their favourite area was the bleak Romney Marsh. This did not stop them from travelling to counties further afield in pursuit of illegal gains.

When the duty on tea was cut in 1745, some of the gang diversified into highway robbery, while others stuck to smuggling. Gin, brandy and tobacco were still highly prized. In the mid-1700s, a four-gallon tub of brandy sold in France for one pound could cost four in England. Naturally, the smugglers indulged themselves at such prices and their behaviour became even rowdier through drink. They would drink in Kentish inns with all their loaded pistols in view on the table and had no mercy for anyone. On 1 April 1746, they escaped with around forty horses belonging to the Folkestone Gang after a joint smuggling venture culminated in a vicious fight over the spoils.

Now violence was on the increase, especially when a brutal leader, Thomas Kingsmill, took over the gang in 1747. The Hawkhurst Gang were known to have bested the revenue men, on one occasion flogging them brutally with coachmen's whips. The unfortunate victims were then sent off in a smuggling vessel headed for France and dumped there – a cruel fate as England and France were at war. Indeed, anyone who tried to thwart the Hawkhurst Gang was dealt with swiftly and without compassion. In Goudhurst, a village south of Maidstone, homes and farms were burnt down and animals and people were slaughtered, although the feisty villagers formed a militia to oppose Thomas Kingsmill. The Goudhurst men fought bravely and managed to oust the usurpers, but most other areas continued to suffer. Informers, or anyone who offended the gang, continued to be threatened, had their houses and crops burnt down and their cattle slaughtered.

The Hawkhurst Gang carried out a number of outrageous brutalities across the county, once falsely accusing a man of stealing two bags of (contraband) tea, a crime for which he was executed. After a particularly brutal murder of two men which took place in Fordingbridge in Hampshire (relating to a squabble over contraband landed in Poole in Dorset) it was announced in January 1749 that a pardon would be given to any smuggler who would provide information instrumental in the capture of the Hawkhurst Gang. As a result, the leaders of the gang were caught and executed. Some were hanged, some both hanged and gibbeted, and one died of a heart attack brought on by fear before the sentence could be carried out. After he was hanged, Thomas Kingsmill's body was hung in chains at Goudhurst.

The violent Aldington Gang worked the entire coastline from Dover and Deal to Rye in Sussex throughout the early 1800s, and was probably comprised of soldiers returning from the French wars. Their base, Aldington, is located at the edge of Romney Marsh. Their nickname was 'The Blues', possibly from the colour of their clothing, and they were led by George Ransley, whose cousins, James and William, were known as the 'Roaring Ransleys'. James and William were smugglers, although they were executed in 1800 at Penenden Heath for highway robbery (see the separate account under 'Gentlemen of the Road'). George Ransley was an extrovert who enjoyed being in charge, organising his men with military precision and never taking unnecessary risks, but he was a fair boss. He retained his own surgeon so someone was on hand if anyone in his gang was hurt, and he tried to look after the injured man's family while the breadwinner was indisposed. In return, he received their loyalty and bought their silence.

When unloading the larger eight-gallon casks of wines and spirits, the gang would use a packhorse. The four-gallon casks were carried away by 'tubmen'. If the customs men were about, a rocket would be used to fire off a warning, and the cargo would be marked with a buoy and tipped over the side into the sea. The way of unloading the tubs was simple but effective. As soon as the lugger arrived, a man would swim out with a line which was pushed through a block. When he swam back with the line, the tubs could be slung over in pairs and hauled to the shore. The Aldington Gang's cargo would then be carted to its own storage place at Hockley Hole (now known as Hockley Sole), located on a stretch of cliffs between Dover and Folkestone.

The Aldington Gang clashed with blockade men in November 1820 at nearby Sandgate when a galley carrying spirits and tobacco was intercepted. Around 250 men, assigned to unload, transport and protect the cargo, attacked two officers and captured another. The smugglers completed their transaction safely and released the captured officer the next day.

Another terrible tale of revenge on a revenue man, attributed to the Aldington Gang, happened near Dover cliff top. The officer's legs were bound together and then he was blindfolded. To his horror, the smugglers told him he was to be thrown over the cliff. Ignoring his cries for mercy, they hauled him to the edge and pushed him over, till he was clinging for his life onto a few grassy clumps. Terrified, he hung there, screaming for someone to rescue him. Just as his grip began to waver, his struggles dislodged his blindfold and he actually dared to look down. The ground was just two feet below him. He'd been clinging on over a chalk pit. No doubt the smugglers were laughing into their beer but at least the officer lived to tell the tale.

The Blues were halted because of a crime that offended common decency and which took place just off Dover beach. Most smugglers actually avoided using Dover because of the high concentration of preventive forces: not only the customs officers, but also the soldiers from the castle. However, the confident Aldington Gang were known to have used Dover beach for their nefarious activities. George himself crossed the Channel regularly on the Dover Packet to obtain brandy, tobacco, tea and lace. His men would be ready to unload the illicit cargo into a false-bottomed boat, which they rowed with muffled oars. There would be extra men, armed, to provide protection.

On 30 July 1826, two blockade officers who were patrolling among the bathing machines saw the gang's boat, which was carrying contraband for landing. The gang had already implemented a number of profitable runs and this time they intended landing on Dover's beach, beneath the castle casements, unaware they had been spotted. The quartermaster, Richard Morgan, fired a shot as a warning to the smugglers or to alert other blockade men. The smugglers fired back and killed him, also injuring his colleague. The dead man was buried in St Martin's churchyard. Unfortunately for 'The Blues', they had slaughtered a popular community figure, and revenge was required. Lt Hellard, an official of the blockade, offered a £500 reward to bring the gang to justice, although this failed to persuade any of the locals to submit evidence. The community, of course, enjoyed the luxuries provided by the smugglers and fear of reprisal must have played a part. Meanwhile, Hellard urged the Bow Street Runners to question suspicious-looking strangers.

Eventually a fellow smuggler came forward with evidence, and a raiding party, together with the Bow Street Runners, went to George Ransley's cottage to Aldington, 'Bourne Tap'. The name derives from the illegal spirits George sold at a high profit. First, the men killed the Ransley's dog, and so found George in his nightshirt, in bed. They handcuffed him and he was arrested together with seven others. Within a few weeks, the blockade men had achieved a score of nineteen captured smugglers, and in January 1827, all were tried at Maidstone Assizes. The smuggler who pulled the trigger on Richard Morgan was named as Richard Wire. Unsurprisingly, all were found guilty, but, thanks to an excellent lawyer, Mr Platt of Ashford, they were transported to Tasmania rather than executed.

If one is cynical, it is possible to theorise that a long trial might have brought up evidence detrimental to those in high places. Further, mass execution may well have aroused further rebellion. In fact, Mr Platt had made an assurance to the Solicitor General that the prisoners would plead guilty on condition the death penalty was not imposed and that they were transported for the remainder of their lives.

The informers were two of the arrested smugglers, Edward Horne and James Bushell, who were let off for their co-operation, although later, Edward Horne was arrested for horse-stealing. A further two informers were William Marsh, who received a £130 reward, and James Spratford, who received £100. James Spratford had once been a smuggler, but in around 1800 he became the parish overseer for Aldington, and he used his training as a one-time signaller in the Navy to inform on George Ransley's activities. It is claimed the women of the village burned Spratford's effigy right in front of his house. Nor would the barber shave him in case he was tempted to slit his throat. With his money, James Spratford bought a horse-drawn threshing machine, but it was destroyed by the labourers in the wages riot of 1830.

Some of the other smugglers escaped the blockade and continued to live in the area. A former smuggler wrote to the *Kentish Express* in 1889 to say that the last member of the Aldington Gang, a one-legged smuggler, had died in 'Black Ditch', a street at the bottom of Military Road in Dover.

As for George, he spent five long years toiling in Tasmania and earned a pardon. He settled in his new country, returning to his former profession, farming, and after his pardon, was able to send for his wife and their nine children. Former convicted fellow-smugglers became his labourers, working around 200 acres of farmland. He lived on happily till his eighties, proving that, sometimes, crime does pay! He died at River Plenty, North Norfolk.

The Deal Smugglers

The Deal boatman worked like an organized 'gang'. They built shallow boats called luggers which could move across the treacherous Goodwin Sands without mishap or fear of pursuit from the Navy's blockade ships or the revenue's cutters. They also used long galleys with a small sail that could speed the thirty or so miles to France in under five hours, with room on board for about thirty men. The galleys had the advantage that they could aim into a head wind, again preventing pursuit. These galleys could even negotiate the Goodwin Sands at a low tide.

On 14 January 1784, William Pitt the Younger ordered the 13th Light Dragoons to move in on the Deal fisherman from Sandwich. But the news reached the Deal smugglers in advance and 300 of them were waiting ready for the confrontation. Fortunately for the Dragoons, reinforcements were sent from Canterbury. Because of recent bad storms, all the boats were pulled up onto the beach, providing an easy target.

Meanwhile, the people of Deal refused the troops lodgings, so they had to stay on a farm that night. The next day, they went to the beach and set fire to all the boats and luggers, holding the people off with their bayonets. The Deal smugglers were halted for the time being, but in a short while they were up and running once again. The rewards were too great to give up. This is easy to understand in view of the following: In 1801, revenue officers raided a post-chaise leaving Deal; they discovered an enormous quantity of French lace and 246 pairs of gloves. In a separate incident, a King's messenger was apprehended bringing in goods from a Deal lugger, a fine collection of silk kerchiefs.

A further incident also occurred in 1801: smugglers called on the Deal locals for help when the revenue forced their lugger onto the beach. The locals confronted the revenue men, attacked them and then boldly brought the cargo ashore, comprising tobacco, cloth and playing cards. But the boundaries were never fixed. Around 1817, when the blockade men attempted to arrest a number of local smugglers, they were set upon by the local people and had to withdraw to seek shelter in a shop. As a result, the mayor of Deal accused the blockade men of assault on the smugglers and ordered their arrest.

Liberty Forever

Dover Town Gaol was erected on the south side of the market place near the Guildhall in 1746. However, in 1820, the town authorities were roundly upstaged by the common people, who managed to breach the gaol. In May of that year, eleven seamen from Sandgate and Folkestone were arrested for smuggling by a revenue officer called Billy 'Hellfire' Lilburn, but an angry crowd of friends and relatives marched to Dover and assembled outside the gaol to demand their release. Throwing rocks and stones at the soldiers, the mob chanted: 'Liberty forever!' Sir Thomas Mantell, the mayor of Dover, read them the Riot Act but the mob wasn't impressed and began to attack the walls of the gaol with picks and crowbars. Because the prisoners were locked in secure cells, the rescue party broke down the doors and severely damaged the prison. Troops were called in but they, too, were pelted with stones and tiles and the mayor was attacked. Billy Lilburn, the arresting officer, tried without success to persuade the commanding officer, said to be the founder of the blockade, 'Flogging Joey' McCullock, to repel the crowd with fire, but he declined.

Blue Plaque in Market Square: the location of the old stocks, pillory and whipping post.

'Flogging Joey' McCulloch in uniform as a young midshipman (by kind permission of Dover District Council).

Gaol Lane, where the old gaol was located.

Eventually, the prisoners were freed and borne away in horse-drawn carriages, stopping off first at the 'Red Cow' pub in Dover to saw off the chains on their hands. They went into hiding and, in this case, the lucky escapees managed to avoid recapture. The town of Dover was subjected to a rampage by the mob, which did as much damage as it could, smashing windows and anything else that got in its way. The gaol had been destroyed by the rescue operation and had to be rebuilt the same year. A new gaol was built at Maison Dieu in 1834, and it is still there in the basement area although it is presently closed to visitors.

The Riot Act of 1715

Riotous behaviour was a serious problem for the civil authorities and, in 1715, the Riot Act was passed, making it a crime for a group of people numbering twelve or more to refuse to disperse within one hour of being ordered to do so by a magistrate. However, as the story above demonstrates, it was actually extremely harrowing for the magistrate to read the Riot Act during violent mob activity.

Decline and Fall

In 1813, 12,000 gallons of illegal brandy were landed at nearby Romney Marsh, so clearly smuggling was still providing a lucrative income for nineteenth-century 'free-traders' as they were – euphemistically – called. However, smuggling had had its heyday. When the war with France ended in 1815, there were more revenue men as well as soldiers available to target the smugglers and a blockade around the Kent coast was implemented. Instead of just confiscating

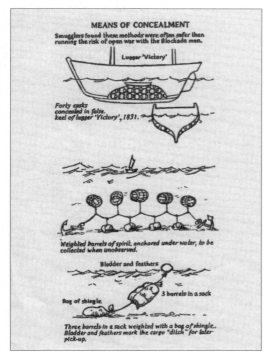

Methods of concealment of contraband (by kind permission of Dover District Council).

goods, the officers were bent on capturing the culprits. Smugglers were forced to become more organised, finding ingenious methods of landing their spoils, burying tubs filled with contraband for collection or using false-bottomed boats. Water tanks were fitted with false sides to hide alcohol while tobacco could be imported by plaiting it into a piece of rope.

However, during 1817, as men returned to England at the end of the Napoleonic Wars, there were fears that the economic hardship fuelled by unemployment was tempting them back into the smuggling trade. The blockade set up by Captain McCulloch extended along the south coast from Sheppey to Sussex. McCulloch supervised things from a man-of-war anchored off Deal and it was a fierce operation – after all, there were 250,000 soldiers returning after Waterloo.

Then, when taxes on many imported goods were abolished in 1831, smuggling was no longer viable and began to decline. For most people the small rewards were simply not worth the risk of capture, although a few continued risking their lives.

The little village of Sholden, near Deal, was also an area of intense smuggling activity. It is claimed there is a smuggler's hide with a secret door leading from the dining room of a Tudor house at Hull Place.

Reformed Deal Boatmen?

On 31 August 1863, a boatman, George Makins, aged fifty-nine, was found guilty of stealing potatoes and a marrow belonging to a John Mantle. Sentenced to seven days in Sandwich Gaol, the Bench made a surprising comment suggesting that it was regrettable that a Deal boatman should be in the prisoner's position; this, it appeared, was a rare situation since that class of men was known for its honesty.

Morality and the Coastguards

It would be reasonable to assume that the revenue men themselves might easily be corrupted by the nature of their work. To this end, prison campaigner Mrs Elizabeth Fry, who already concerned herself with helping to improve the morality of sailors, extended her efforts in 1836 to the revenue men (now known as coastguards). A report dated 1 February of that year, says: 'Each station in the three Kingdoms has been furnished, at her own expense, with a library for the use of the crew of the station, consisting of from fifty to sixty volumes of cheap works, mostly of a moral and religious tendency'.

Mrs Fry was honest enough to reply to *The Times* on 3 February, explaining that these books were not at her own expense. The Government, her friends and the public provided the money.

III

WRECKING AND SALVAGE – DOVER'S OPPORTUNISTS

Save a stranger from the sea
And he'll turn your enemy
(Old seafaring superstition)

'Man or Beast' Rule

There were two kinds of lawbreaking loosely defined as 'wrecking' or 'levelling' in the vernacular of the time. There are a few reports of wreckers deliberately luring ships into hazardous waters in order to plunder them, using false signals with misplaced lights and sounding foghorns. However, due to sparse concrete evidence, there are differences of opinion among historians about how widespread this practice was, leading some to the conclusion that most wreckers were simple opportunists who regarded the spoils of shipwrecks as a natural product of the sea's bounty. These opportunists were skilled in stripping wrecked vessels under the noses of the receivers.

Henry III first put forward the 'man or beast' rule, which meant that if any man or beast escaped alive from a foundered vessel, it was not to be considered a wreck. But the regard for property was higher than that for human life and the crews of foundered vessels about to be plundered were, it is claimed, sometimes slaughtered so the wreckers could benefit within the confines of the law. If they weren't actually murdered, then it was certainly not in the wreckers' best interests to help them. Later, Henry's son, Edward I, continued to uphold the 'man or beast' rule, although it was repealed in 1771. In the nineteenth century, the Receiver of Wrecks was established to deal with claims, but they too valued property more highly than life.

Between Deal and Dover stands the South Foreland lighthouse, overlooking a part of the white cliffs of Dover. The main danger to shipping is not the white cliffs or the hazards of reefs and rocks as one might expect, but the treacherous Goodwin Sands, those shifting tidal islands lying three miles offshore in one of the world's busiest shipping lanes. Situated as they are in the Strait of Dover, they prove a hazard to the shore from Ramsgate to Deal, although they stop short of Dover. Despite this, Dover has had its share of wrecks and its inhabitants have participated in the exploitation of vessels foundering on the sands. Indeed, so many vessels have perished in the area that it has been described as the 'shippe swallower'. Even the largest of vessels could disappear without trace within an hour, swallowed by the greedy quicksands to settle on the chalk bed below. It is claimed that more than 3,000 wrecks lie beneath the sands

Pub signs celebrate Dover's sometimes sinister maritime past.

in this part of the Channel, although some estimates are more conservative at about half that number. Between the sands and the shore, a deep layer of water known as The Downs provides anchorage for ships, safely reached at high tide.

Sometimes, the same men would act as both lifeboat crew and wreckers, genuinely intent on saving life, while not being averse to cheating the receiver by carrying off some of the booty for themselves; a booty to which they believed they were entitled – after all, much of their livelihood depended on smuggling and wrecking.

An Early Example of Community Service

There is a charming story, dated around 1367, about how certain felons could be granted some remission of their punishment in return for a special service, a striking similarity with our modern-day 'community service' penalty system for petty criminals. A hermit monk called Nicholas de Legh, who lived at St Margaret's Bay, set up his own light at the top of the cliff to warn passing ships. This was a common practice also undertaken by monasteries and priories. Certain felons who were prepared to help feed and support the monk were granted forty days of remission. So the kind holy hermit spent his time maintaining his light and praying for those in peril, duly supported by the local criminal fraternity.

Too Late Now!

In 1634, a proper lighthouse at South Foreland was proposed, but the Corporation of Trinity House objected. A lighthouse here, and another at North Foreland, was unnecessary and dangerous, said the corporation, and an additional light would guide England's enemies into The Downs. They claimed that wreckers, those who deliberately lured ships to their destruction in order to salvage and steal the cargo, would take advantage by displaying false lights. Also, it would be expensive. Fortunately, King Charles I pulled rank, and a lighthouse was erected at South Foreland to warn ships off the Goodwin Sands. Later, the North Foreland lighthouse also went ahead. The lighthouses proved profitable due to the toll imposed on shipping, and the corporation decided it wanted them back, but the King refused.

Beating the System

In the 1630s, the toll amounted to one halfpenny per ton of cargo on passing shipping. However, there was some deliberate cheating. The harbour master collected the tolls for the lighthouse owner when the ships docked, and would be paid a percentage. If he considered the lighthouse owner wasn't handing over a fair sum for his efforts, he would send the tolls to another lighthouse in the area. William Bullock at Dungeness received a toll which should have been paid to Sir John Meldrun at South Foreland, and it is claimed Bullock kept the money for himself.

Wrecking Rights

During the Middle Ages, there were lengthy disputes about who was entitled to the gains from wrecks on the Goodwin Sands. The Lord Warden of the Cinque Ports claimed, in 1602, that the rights were his, but the Crown believed it was entitled to everything. The lords of the manors, who owned extensive areas of the coast, asserted hereditary rights to the spoils as well as various privileges bestowed on their families in earlier times. These disagreements caused endless legal disputes, keeping the courts busy. In 1613, the clerk of Dover Castle, together with William Ward of the Admiralty of the Cinque Ports, and the Droit Gatherer General, was accused of embezzling the profits of wrecked ships. In their defence, all of them claimed they were the rightful beneficiaries.

In 1616, the mayor of Dover made a statement, claiming the rights of the Lord Warden's Admiralty jurisdiction over all cargo salvaged from wrecks.

Cannibalism at Sea

A vessel foundered in the early sixteenth century off Dover; tragically, famine had resulted in cannibalism, and the distressed crew were unable to resist a storm off the South Foreland. The ship went down with all her crew, and the Dovorians made off with the valuable cargo.

Get out of My Boat!

It was a depressing time for the British at the end of the eighteenth century, uncertain of the future and dependent on the British Navy to keep Napoleon Bonaparte from invading our shores. The Straits were busy, as ships sought safe anchorage in the deep water of The Downs while the usual traffic of trade continued as before. Many ships of all nationalities came to grief on the Goodwin Sands, and the natural consequence of this was a renewed surge of wrecking.

A West Indiaman, the *Endeavour*, loaded with rum, sugar and coffee at an estimated value of £23,000 foundered on the Goodwins on its homeward journey at 3.00 a.m. on 8 February 1805. The cargo was owned jointly by the *Endeavour*'s owner, Mr Henry Wildman, who ran an estate in Jamaica, and his agent and passenger, John Kneller.

At daybreak, a Deal boatman, Peter Atkins, climbed aboard offering to help land the cargo safely; after all, the ship clearly was beyond saving. Peter Atkins signalled to the shore, and a horde of Deal boatmen raced to the ship's side and boarded, then began to break open the hatches for the spoils. The first cargo they took off was a large quantity of rum which found its way into Atkins' boat, *The Noble*. Three times Peter Atkins made the journey from the *Endeavour* to the beach. During the last trip, just as night was falling, the boat carried hogsheads of sugar which were the property of Henry Wildman, some sugar belonging to John Kneller and the *Endeavour*'s compass.

Suddenly, Peter Atkins told John Kneller to get out of his boat and into another and, as might be expected, not much of the haul reached Mr Iggulden, the agent at Deal. Henry Wildman's son was alarmed when he heard that only £500 worth of cargo had been delivered. He arrived to make enquiries, and he and John Kneller interrogated Peter Atkins, both at the agent's office and, later, in the Three Kings Inn. Atkins roundly denied ever being near the scene of the wreck. On being pressed, he changed his story; everything had been surrendered – except for one small cask of rum which he'd kept for himself on the last trip. He meant to sell it, he said, so the owners would not need to pay duty, and he had shared some coffee with his crew.

The police and the customs officers were brought in, and on 17 February, Peter Atkins' house in Beach Street, Deal, was raided. Two sacks of sugar were found, but Atkins was missing. A warrant was issued for his arrest, but what the authorities did not suspect was that their quarry had hidden in the attic of his house. In a later attempt to arrest him, the Bow Street Runners were repelled by the loyal Deal boatmen, and it took the efforts of the local cavalry unit to arrest the elusive wrecker, who eventually appeared for trial at the Old Bailey on 26 June.

Within fifteen minutes, the jury found him guilty of felony and piracy and plundering the cargo of the ship *Endeavour*, and he was sentenced to death. However, his wife was housekeeper to Lady Hester Stanhope at Walmer Castle, and Elizabeth Atkins swiftly persuaded her mistress to help her husband. The lucky wrecker was saved from hanging when his sentence was changed to transportation. Once in Brazil, he worked for the Admiralty in Rio de Janeiro for a while, then he moved twice more, to Guernsey and then to Calais. During the mid-1800s he returned Deal where he eventually died in his eighties.

Every Man for Himself

A looting incident occurred shortly after an East Indiaman (a large ship engaged in trade with the East Indies), *The North*, came to grief near Dover on 30 August 1866. *The North*, a ship of 1,238 tons, having set off from Liverpool loaded with coal for Aden, took on a cargo of rice in Burma for the return journey. But the vessel got into difficulty on the Goodwin Sands and, as it was dark, seventeen of the crew abandoned ship in the lifeboat while the remaining fourteen boarded the pinnace (a ship's small sailing or rowing boat). Those in the lifeboat were helped to safety at Dover, and the fourteen in the pinnace landed in Deal. Naturally, the distressed men had been unable to rescue any of their cargo or personal belongings.

At dawn there was great excitement along the coast and a great number of boats set off from the shore. Men from every town and village in the area wanted to be there to pick over the wreckage and make a quick profit. They clambered onto the vessel and stripped it of everything they could find, not only the personal belongings of the crew including clothing, food and tools, but also the ship's sails, her instruments, her rope, her wire, her blocks, shackles and deadeyes (a circular wooden block with a groove around the circumference to take a lanyard). As the tide went out and the lower hull was exposed, they even dismantled most of the copper sheathing and took it away in their boats. They had some security in the knowledge that soon the ship would be claimed by the Goodwins and disappear forever.

The men of Dover, Deal and the surrounding villages had committed a serious crime. The Merchant Shipping Act specified that salvaged goods should be protected and returned to their rightful owner if possible. If the men had returned the goods to the receiver, their actions would have been applauded.

Soon, certain goods, for example the valuable canvas and rope, were found in the possession of Dennis and Dowell, Dover marine dealers. Other dealers implicated were Fosters at Deal and a papermaking business in the nearby village of River. Some of the written records of these businesses were negligible, and everyone concerned feigned ignorance of who had been involved and what had happened. Once again, the seafaring community had closed ranks.

A Board of Trade enquiry was held and the results reported to the House of Commons. There was a suspicion that even the coastguards had been implicated in this unsavoury incident. Certain officials were stripped of their duties, there were a few convictions, and then the matter came to a close and most of the wreckers went free, unpunished.

Illegal Salvage

The Times on 27 April 1909 ran a report about a man who was stopped while pushing a hawker's cart in Dover. In the cart were two chests of tea, amounting to 170lbs: the hawker said he'd discovered the haul on the Deal sand-hills. On 6 April, he was charged with possessing shipwrecked goods and intending to defraud the revenue, and he was fined £9 9s – or one month in gaol.

The authorities had concluded the man's haul came from the four-masted passenger steamer, the *Mahratta* of the Brocklebank Line, which was wrecked on her return journey from Calcutta with her cargo of 10,000 tons of rubber, rice, tea and jute, ninety crew and seventeen passengers. The *Mahratta* strayed from her course on 8 April 1909, and struck Fork Spit on the Goodwin Sands. Captain Ellery did all he could to refloat the ship, but without success. About a hundred local men were engaged on a commission basis to start saving the cargo (thirty-three per cent of the cargo successfully landed).

The following day, Good Friday, lifeboats were launched to help the steamer, but she was stuck fast. Two sturdy tugs were dispatched from Dover to assist a number of other tugs, but their combined efforts failed to shift the steamer. Some of the passengers were landed at Deal Pier by the lifeboats, and the local boatmen continued to take off the cargo and luggage to enable the ship to be floated. But, at 9.00 a.m. on 11 April, the stricken *Mahratta* broke in two as her plates buckled and her iron rivets broke apart. The men working on her, who were trying to jettison jute while up to their waists in water, steeled themselves for a possible explosion. Eventually, heavy seas further damaged the *Mahratta* and what was left of her listed over, gradually sinking. The chief engineer, Samuel Gibson, was so distraught that he cut his own throat and was found dead in his cabin. Later, the Board of Trade inquiry blamed the pilot for not recognizing the Gull Light when he saw it, despite its presence being reported to him by the second mate. His failure resulted in the ship taking a wrong course. Lightships were introduced as an additional navigational aid during the early 1800s: the Gull Light came into operation in 1809, and was anchored on the western side of the Goodwin Sands.

Dover's forty-six feet high Prince of Wales Lighthouse dates from 1902 and is still operational (by kind permission of The Prince of Wales Sea Training School).

Although the hawker in Dover with his contraband tea was eventually caught and punished, it is a matter for conjecture how many boatmen actually managed to keep the full hundred per cent of their landed cargo, rather than the thirty-three per cent to which they were entitled.

Another Mahratta!

A terrible coincidence occurred on 6 October 1939, when *The Mahratta*, an East India ship with a cargo of tea and goatskins, came to grief in the same spot as the *Mahratta* lost in 1909. Every Deal boat turned up to try to help with the salvage operations. Again, booty disappeared – and again it was chests of tea.

Locals went around the town trying to sell the contraband tea, and they did rather well since tea was rationed at the time. But HM Customs was on the trail of the missing tea, making enquiries among the local community. The men began to panic and, in their desperation to avoid capture, they flushed the tea down the lavatories. When people emptied their sinks and baths of hot water, the tea began to swell in the drainage system, so that soon the pipes of North Deal were completely blocked.

IV

PRESS GANGS

Imagine the terror of being physically torn from your friends and family and everything familiar and precious to you. Your captors are a bunch of swarthy bullies and you are being hauled to an evil place, thick with pestilence and filthy smells. You know that this will be your prison for the time being, a dank, dark hole, where you are trapped behind an iron grating firmly secured by an iron bar and a padlock. You become part of a disgusting mass of writhing human bodies, all as terrified as you are, screaming and fighting and cursing and, like you, smelling of fear.

You haven't murdered anyone, assaulted anyone, or even stolen a miserable loaf of bread. On the contrary, your only crime is to be a seaman. You have fallen victim to the horrible and entirely legal practice of the Press Gang, for the British Navy was desperate for men. Press Gangs operated in Dover; in fact, they plied their trade in human misery in fifty ports around the British coastline. The only exemption accepted by the Admiralty were foreigners, who were excused by a law passed in 1740, although later this was modified to permit aliens to be pressed if they had served on a British merchant ship for at least two years. Foreigners were also liable if they had married a British woman, and it is claimed some unfortunate seamen were pressed on their honeymoons. Sometimes foreigners unfamiliar with the English language remained in the Royal Navy because they were unable to insist upon seeing a consul. Documents of release for successful applicants carried a detailed description of the man on the back to avoid their being sold to a non-exempted seaman.

Each major port had a captain, who was paid one pound a day, and each smaller port employed a lieutenant (five shillings a day plus two shillings and ninepence subsistence). In 1799, the captain at Dover was Benjamin Hulke. Senior officers, like captains and lieutenants, were called Regulating Officers, and the headquarters of the local Impress Service was known as 'the Rendezvous'. Each would supervise a midshipman and gangs of men. Sometimes a bargain would be made with the gangers, promising them exemption in return for their services as pressmen.

Once the gangs were known by the Dover locals, lookouts were stationed along the coast to give warning if one of the King's ships anchored nearby. Pressmen were forced to roam the surrounding villages, since most of the qualified seamen would have taken off to hide elsewhere. The gangers received 'road money' of one penny a mile, while officers did a little better with three. Those captured were first escorted and imprisoned in the Rendezvous until the Regulating Officer could take a look at them to certify them for service. If a man tried to plead infirmity or illness, the local surgeon would examine him for a shilling. As soon as the Articles of War had been read to the unfortunate seaman – whether or not he was in any state to hear or understand them – then he was in the service of the King. No provision whatsoever would

A Skull and crossbones. Since the 1850s, the death's head, or skull and crossbones, has been used to label poisonous substances. It was also a symbol for black-flagged pirate ships.

be made for his abandoned family. Once a seaman had been pressed into the service, however unwillingly, insubordination would be harshly punished by flogging or even execution.

Ruthless locals became informers for a reward or for the sake of settling a dispute. It was dangerous for young men to be fast with the affections of the local women, or for a man to be unfaithful to his wife. It was also dangerous if a man had the seaman's distinctive rolling gait, which picked him out for pressing.

When the Navy was especially desperate for hands, the gangers' pay went up. Their power was enormous; one word and a man's fate was sealed – a stint in the Royal Navy that could last for many years. Those rich enough could bribe the officers with goods or money, but for the poor, the only prospect was that dank, dark prison in the bowels of a Royal Navy ship prior to setting sail for the high seas.

V

GENTLEMEN OF THE ROAD

'Never desert my companions in time of danger, confess nothing if taken … be ready day or night to answer the call … be faithful to my companions in all their designs and attempts … and never fly from an equal number of opposers but die courageously.'
(Some sentiments from 'The Highwayman's Oath')

Most people probably have a romantic view of a highwayman's life. Much glamorised on the Hollywood screen, it is claimed that most highway robbery was committed in England. The practice began around the fourteenth century although the term 'highwayman' was not used until the seventeenth century. Many foreigners complained about England's lawlessness.

Some highwaymen of note were actually the sons of the upper-middle classes. The problem of their activities was exacerbated because a culture of bribery and corruption was endemic in the country. To some degree, England became rather proud of its gentlemen of the road, and soon tales of their exploits were exchanged across the tables of the gentry. Again, foreigners were not impressed at the manner in which the English regarded their highwaymen as heroes. It is true that on occasion these so-called 'gentlemen' were vicious and might rape the women or cut off a lady's finger for her ring. There is even one instance of a gang of highwaymen breaking into a house where they raped the lady of the manor and her daughter. However, the main motive was that of profit, and deliberate murder or personal bodily harm was rare.

Kent had more highway robbery than any other part of England except for the county of Essex, and the practice reached its peak during the sixteenth and seventeenth centuries. Highwaymen's activities were, of course, always undertaken away from the sharp eyes of the law, so there are few cases in the vicinity of Dover town with its soldiers and customs law enforcement. However, highwaymen were to be found on quiet Kentish roads close to Dover. Out in the countryside, wooded areas lent secrecy, and the rutted muddy state of roads hindered the passing of carriages, helping to make the highwayman's crime and his escape on horseback across the open fields less likely to be detected. A concealed flintlock pistol and a bag to carry the booty and any brutal young fortune-hunter could be in business. In the 1700s Sholden, near Deal, was a lawless place, teeming with highwaymen and footpads (a felon who ambushed and robbed travellers on foot), and nearby Great Mongeham and Little Mongeham were also known as a hotbed for their activities.

Highwaymen obtained their information about possible targets from publicans who often played the role of 'fence'. A highwayman was described then as a 'Black Robin,' probably derived from the Robin Hood legend.

A Legend of Their Time

There were two highwaymen from Ruckinge, near Hythe, who were brothers or cousins to George Ransley, the leader of the Aldington Gang of smugglers. The coastal territory of the smugglers stretched from Dover to Rye in Sussex, and since Kent was thick with highwaymen, people travelling to Dover never knew when they would be commanded to 'stand and deliver' by George's young relatives, who were known in the surrounding area as 'the rascally brothers'. James Finn, a parish clerk who knew the brothers when the family lived at Merstham, records that they were fine-looking men, but disregarded the Sabbath and practised every degree of immorality, including playing cards, dice and dominoes!

Their career was short but productive in criminal terms; besides highway robbery and smuggling, they committed burglary, horse-stealing and common assault. The last may allude to an attempt to shoot at a certain Elizabeth Gurr. As a result, on 20 August 1800 the two young men were hanged at Penenden Heath near Maidstone, loudly lamenting their sinful lives and showing all due contrition.

Their sister Elizabeth was driven to despair. Overcome by the tragic deaths of her brothers before their thirtieth birthdays, she hanged herself in her room. How terrible for their quiet, law-abiding parents, also to lose their daughter by hanging. However, it is doubtful whether Elizabeth was such an innocent; it is claimed that the Ransley girls played their part in relieving travelling folk of their valuables just as their brothers did, and that the three sisters frequently worked the infamous Ashford to Hythe road. The boys' father personally collected their bodies, returning them to Ruckinge for burial.

Choosing a Territory

Between Deal and Dover, highwaymen used to wait for the stagecoach to approach a long hill up to Ringwould. As soon as the stagecoach was forced to slow down, the highwaymen would ambush it. This part of the road, Oxney Bottom, is also known as Haunted Highway because the ghost of one of the highwaymen is claimed to haunt it.

Escape by Samphire

One highwayman destined for imprisonment in Dover Castle in 1768 demonstrated incredible bravery, both in escaping his captors and by grasping an opportunity when he saw it while talking to his guards on Dover's magnificent cliff tops. On Wednesday 1 June 1768, he ambushed a butcher not far from Woodnesborough. Mr Philip Harriotson, a wealthy tradesman, had been doing business in Ash. Mounted on a bay mare, the robber presented his pistol and on demand, the butcher surrendered his purse, a gold watch, a ring and a small box containing valuables such as medals and foreign coins. As the highwayman made off, he caught his hair (a wig) in tree branches which gave Mr Harriotson the opportunity to strike the pistol from his hand with his whip. The highwaymen struck the butcher and galloped off, but he was pursued by Mr Harriotson who overtook him, unseating him. It was a plucky effort on the part of the butcher, but unfortunately the highwayman managed to get back into his saddle and escape, while his pursuer was thrown from his own horse.

Mr Harriotson later described the highwayman as disfigured by smallpox and missing the little finger of his left hand. It was a satisfactory description because the man was caught the next day at the Silver Lion in Dover. A group of four men managed to outwit him by pretending to be friendly, drinking and talking to him. Two pistols and a poignard were concealed on his

Samphire grew on Dover's cliffs, where a highwayman once escaped.

body, and the butcher's money was in his waistcoat pocket. Altogether it amounted to £60 in £20 banknotes, forty guineas in cash as well as the valuables.

Subsequently, he was found to be a German by the name of James Frederick Hellick and exhibited due remorse at his trial. He was to be sent to Dover Castle pending transport to Maidstone Jail. Hellick chatted in a friendly way with the escort of five constables as the party climbed the hill to the castle. He requested a moment to watch the samphire-gatherers working the cliff face, and the constables agreed. Here, rock samphire, an unprepossessing plant with smallish yellow florets, once grew in abundance on the cliff face. It had tasty leaves, said to be similar to asparagus, which were gathered, cooked and eaten by the locals, and also sent to London where it was regarded as a delicacy. The dangerous activity of collecting the leaves was achieved by lowering oneself on a rope down the cliff face.

The gatherers left work for a break but left their ropes fixed to posts at the top of the cliff. The temptation was overpowering, for the ropes reached right to the shore – and safety. Using a popular trick, Hellick suddenly pointed in the opposite direction, as though he had spotted some amazing sight. The constables turned – and the resourceful felon took his chance by grasping a rope and descending to the shore. He had escaped before the slow-witted constables realised and was never to see the inside of Dover Castle's prison walls.

Hangman's Lane

The inhabitants of the pretty village of Ringwould saw some terrible sights during medieval times when it was a large and important village. The name Ringwould means a ring of woods, derived from a ring of trees surrounding the village. These trees, no doubt, provided cover for a number of illegal or wicked practices, but Ringwould was prepared.

At the junction of Hangman's Lane with two other roads was the gibbet. The position of this horrible equipment at an intersection of roads was deliberate, and was an extra punishment visited on those who committed serious crimes such a highway robbery or sheep-stealing; the victim would die knowing that after death, his spirit would be confused by the different routes available to it and would not find its way. The bodies of the victims were left in a metal cage until they rotted, or the crows picked them clean.

The village of Ringwould is on the A258 between Dover and Deal, and it is claimed its origins can be traced back 2,000 years. One of the oldest coins ever found in Kent came from Ringwould.

Above: *Hangman's Lane Junction was a place of execution for felons.*

Left: *Hangman's Lane road sign.*

The Decline of the Highwayman

Foreigners were appalled, not only at the activities of the highwaymen, but also by how they were treated. They were hung from the gibbet complete with wigs, their bodies coated with tar to prevent decomposition, just as unfortunate smugglers were.

Eventually highway robbery began to decline and there were very few cases in the 1800s when the rascally Ransleys met their end. The last recorded incident occurred around 1838 following the establishment of the Metropolitan Police in 1829 and the subsequent implementation of a horse patrol on the most important roads of Kent.

Footpads and their decoys

The highwayman's day was done by around the 1830s; instead, petty crime on the road was practised by footpads who often worked in twos or threes, one of whom would capture the victim, while the other/s carried out the robbery. Sometimes a pretty young woman was used as a distraction to give these small gangs the opportunity to pounce and disable their victims.

In early December 1768, the master of an oyster smack at Dover Pier was travelling from Deal to Dover. Mr John Thornhill was robbed by two footpads in Broadlees Bottom, about one mile from Dover Castle. The robbers wore blue greatcoats and Dutch caps and were around five feet nine inches tall. It is recorded that one had a wig while the other sported his own short hair. Having seized their target by his collar, they hurled him onto his back. One threw himself on top of Mr Thornhill while the other went through his pockets for the contents, fourteen guineas in a yellow bag and a watch supplied by John Lelliot at Havant. They even took his fine shoes with their silver-plated buckles, and the unfortunate man had to make his way back to Dover barefoot.

VI

POACHERS, PICKPOCKETS AND SHEEP-STEALERS

Those who claim that petty crimes such as poaching and picking pockets were closely linked to poverty are right – up to a point. Much poaching, for example, was not professional or profit-motivated, but was more likely to be an attempt to put a decent meal on the table for a family: however, this was not necessarily always the case. In eighteenth and nineteenth-century England, a number of middle-class people and those who were part of the gentry were engaged in the practice of poaching, while organised gangs killed game to sell on to butchers and publicans.

Generally, people were tolerant about poaching, viewing it almost as the Englishman's right to partake of the natural bounty of the island, regardless of whose land it occupied. This attitude made poaching more or less acceptable, especially as it helped keep prices down. Poor people who lived in the same area probably would not poach from each other, although criminal gangs might raid a peasant's land as well as that of the landowner.

To be a little cynical, people probably found it easier to tolerate a certain crime when they were unlikely to find themselves its victims – as with smugglers' and wreckers' communities. Therefore, those who poached from rich landowners would be accepted in the local community rather than those who engaged in sheep-stealing or robbery. Even so, the awful punishment for a poor sheep-stealer might be the death penalty, and so the distinctions are endlessly blurred when discussing social and organised crime in these hard times.

Caught in Dover

A man called Powell made his living as a poacher in east Kent during the 1840s. His special skill was escaping – a useful talent for a petty criminal with a very bad reputation. Once he got away from a constable at Bridge, allegedly running the whole distance to Canterbury. At Wingham, near Canterbury, in November 1843, Powell was apprehended by Mr Brenchley, a gamekeeper, who took hold of him. Immediately Powell bit Mr Brenchley and sped off although Brenchley's assistant, Booth, pursued him for some distance. When Booth finally caught him, Powell bit the assistant's thumb and simply vanished again. In December 1843, he was confronted poaching trout, but again, he escaped.

Powell was finally caught in Charlton, near Dover, and although he threatened his captor with a knife, he was arrested. This must have been a relief for east Kent's gamekeepers since Powell's exploits had been told across the county and even in those poaching-tolerant times, he was always described as a 'rogue'.

Swell Mob

When the railways opened and people were able to travel freely, the Swell Mob – or pickpockets – came into their own. The movement of people meant a proliferation of events such as markets, race meetings and public executions, all ideal hunting grounds for the pickpockets who took pains to dress as grandly as the rest of the crowd so as to avoid suspicion.

Not so Nifty-Fingered!

The *Dover Express* reported such a case on Friday, 26 April 1867, claimed to have occurred the previous Saturday. James Douglas was charged with attempting to pick the pocket of a Mr Odden Hambrook but he didn't make a very good job of it.

Mr Hambrook was walking along Snargate Street and when he reached a narrow part of the pavement, he was hustled by James Douglas while an accomplice pressed him on his other side to distract him. Turning around, he felt Douglas' hand going into his pocket and when he looked, he saw the prisoner withdraw his hand. The accomplice escaped but Mr Hambrook managed to get hold of James Douglas and restrain him.

PC Short also appeared as a witness and said he knew the prisoner well as an 'associate of thieves'. What is more, Douglas habitually attended fairs, races and 'places of that sort', where pocket-picking was rife. The magistrate sent James Douglas to prison for one month.

A Young Father in Distress

The *Cinque Ports Herald* of 1826 reports a crime at Sutton, near Dover, which was committed by a young and desperate father of six children. William Newing was tried for stealing a sheep from Richard Marsh. In court, Richard Marsh claimed, 'I live at Ripple. On 13 April, I had some sheep at Sutton. On the morning of the 15th I missed one. I traced it in the direction of the prisoner's house. I searched his house and found it in four quarters, recently cut up'.

Marsh agreed he already knew the prisoner. Then the second witness, Richard Marsh's brother, took the stand and claimed that he found the skin in the cow house under some dung. When the prisoner arrived home, the witness said a sheep had been lost and it was suspected that William Newing had stolen it. At first the prisoner denied that he had anything to do with the crime, and then he retracted, saying that he was sorry for what he'd done. He pleaded with the witness to take the mutton away and not report him, but the witness refused.

A constable, Henry Dixon, showed the court the skin that was found at the prisoner's house and confirmed it was the property of Richard Marsh. The confession of the prisoner was produced before the magistrate. Neither of the brothers had anything to say in William Newing's favour, even though the prisoner tried to explain he was in the greatest distress in trying to feed his children. He was found guilty and mercy was recommended because of his family. However, a verdict of sentence of death was recorded.

The Secret in the Cellar

According to the *Dover Telegraph* in a report dated Saturday 7 January 1843, an eighteen-year-old man, Frederick Price, was charged with stealing four sheep and one lamb from Mr David Dray. The prosecutor, Mr Dickenson, called on Mr Dray, a butcher, to state his case. David Dray said that on 9 December, he noticed that the sheep were no longer in his field and that the lock of the gate had been broken.

On 17 December, there were some sheep for sale at the prisoner's shop and he recognised them as his own animals, especially because there was also a lamb; it was unusual to kill a young lamb at that time of the year. Also, he noticed some skins at the yard of a Mr Humphrey Humphreys and, on inspection, the marks on the skins were similar to those on the sheep that had been lost. The marks were in the form of a 'tiver' between the shoulders, and the letter 'G'. One of the sheep had a black mark on its ear which he had noticed on purchasing the animals. He confirmed that the sheep had been last seen safe in the field located at East Brook on the 8 December. Mr Humphreys, a tanner, said that two people brought the four sheepskins to him on the 14 December and he paid twelve shillings for them. However, he could not remember what they looked like, although he thought Frederick Price was guilty. He was warned to take notice in future of persons trying to sell him skins.

Price claimed he had purchased the sheep at Canterbury Market, but when asked, admitted he didn't know who had driven them home. A woman, Sophie Newman, explained that the prisoner lived in her home and that she remembered him bringing some sheep back on the Thursday night, a fortnight before Price was arrested. Frederick Price had put the sheep in the cellar, where he normally killed his meat. The prisoner had requested Mrs Newman's husband to help him to 'dress' the sheep.

Mr Newman was the next witness, and he confirmed that he and his wife lived on the commercial quay. Mr Newman said that he had agreed to hang up two sheep for a shilling; he stated that two sheep had already been killed, one was alive in the coal cellar, and two more were alive upstairs, one of which was the lamb. All the sheep were very fat with red marks on their shoulders, similar to the one he later saw at the station. He had also told the prisoner he should feed the sheep, but Frederick Price replied that his father kept pigs for a fortnight without feeding them.

Then the skins were produced in court. In spite of an impassioned appeal made by the defence to the jury on Price's behalf, followed by the summing up of the evidence, the jury returned a guilty verdict and Frederick Price was sentenced to transportation for ten years. The paper noted that the court was crowded to excess during the above proceedings.

In 1832, the crimes of cattle, horse and sheep-stealing were reduced to non-capital offences, which is why William Newing was sentenced to death for a lesser crime than that of Frederick Price, who managed to escape with his life. Other crimes removed from the threat of the death penalty were sacrilege, letter-stealing and returning from transportation (1834/5), forgery and coining (1836), burglary and theft from a dwelling house (1837), rape (1841), and attempted murder (1861).

It is claimed the last man caught stealing sheep was hanged at the bottom end of Tower Hamlets in the late nineteenth century.

VII

MURDER AT THE MAISON DIEU

Part of this story was reported in the *Dover Mercury* of 1 June, 2004. The background is true to historical events, although according to records, William of Orange originally intended to land in the north of England. What is certain is that his fleet passed through the Straits of Dover and was caught in a storm. The remainder of the story has been passed down through Dover folklore. The ghost of Mary, companion to Thomas Papillon's wife, is claimed to haunt the Maison Dieu.

In 1688, the Agent Victualler, who resided with his family at Maison Dieu House, was Thomas Papillon, who remained in the post until 1668 and represented Dover in Parliament from 1673-1685. In October of 1688, Thomas' wife became disturbed by the strange behaviour of her husband who had started going out at all hours and had tried to persuade her and the children to leave for their country home at Acrise. She wondered if it was something to do with an attractive woman she had glimpsed at the back entrance to the house the previous evening. She confided in her companion Mary, and asked her to spy on Thomas to see what he was up to.

Mary hid and her patience was rewarded when she spotted a figure in a hooded cloak. The woman let down her hood and revealed her face, and Mary recognised her as someone from the castle. She heard the woman explaining to Thomas that the Dutchman Prince William of Orange was planning to take the throne from James II. William of Orange and his wife Mary were cousins, both being grandchildren of Charles I. Mary was the daughter of the reigning King, James II.

James' forty-year-old Queen, Mary of Modena, was said to have produced a son, a claim disputed by some, who said the childless royal couple had arranged for a baby boy to be brought to the Queen in a warming pan. Whether or not this was true, the boy would be next in line for the throne, displacing Mary of Orange. William of Orange needed to act quickly if he was to secure the throne for his wife and help England to remain Protestant.

The prospect of William's invasion was welcomed by many important Protestants in England who were in league with the Dutch prince. They promised support if he invaded since they were tired of the unpredictable behaviour of James II, and feared a return to Catholicism with the birth of the new child, scornfully described as 'The Pretender.' Now William was expected to arrive from Holland the following evening, at the invitation of seven influential men. The castle was already prepared for his arrival, and Thomas agreed that William of Orange should be brought to Maison Dieu House as already planned.

Maison Dieu House.

Mary hurried to her mistress to tell her the dramatic news, and when Thomas returned, Madame Papillon informed him that she would to go to the Acrise residence with the children presumably because hospitality towards William of Orange would be an act of treason and dangerous. The sixteenth-century red-brick mansion in the little village of Acrise had been passed down to Thomas by his father, David. So, the next day, Madame Papillon, Mary, the children and the servants left Maison Dieu House as arranged, with all their personal belongings. Then the eldest child complained he had forgotten something and asked to go back and get it.

Mary went into the house alone and climbed up to the attic where she glanced out of the window and spotted the young woman from the castle. Soldiers had bound her by her wrists and now they were hiding in the garden, but there was no sign of Thomas. Intrigued and a little scared, Mary went to the room where she had hidden the day before and waited to see what happened. She heard people entering the house and next moment the door burst open and, in a blast of musket fire, Mary fell to the floor. She died from her wounds.

Bad weather delayed William of Orange's arrival in England until early November 1688 (variously reported as the 3 and 5 November). In any case a storm blew him off course in the Dover Straits, to the disappointment of his waiting Protestant supporters, and he finally landed at Torbay. Thomas Papillon went into exile in Holland for his own safety, returning to England to represent the town after things had settled down. William's success in deposing James became known as 'The Glorious Revolution'. James tried to make a comeback with help from Louis XIV of France, but was defeated by William at the Battle of the Boyne in Ireland in 1690.

The former King James II was exiled to France, and Mary, the heir to James' throne, insisted her husband become King rather than merely her regent. The Dutchman William of Orange, unhealthy, asthmatic, but a highly intelligent man and gifted linguist, became England's King William III and reigned until he died after falling from his horse in 1702.

The Papillon residence at Acrise was partly renovated by a descendent in 1955, and the part-Norman church of St Martins contains memorials to a number of deceased Papillons.

VIII

IMMORALITY, DRUNKEN BEHAVIOUR AND PROSTITUTION

Immorality, of course, is not always a criminal offence, and the very concept of what is immoral and what is acceptable depends on the time in which we live as well as the culture prevailing in our local environment. There are also the serious social pressures. Soldiers away from home will still be young men with young men's desires, while prostitutes may be unfortunate young women who have no other way to earn their living than on the streets. Therefore, some of the following cases appertain to the morality of their time and place, and not all of them were necessarily indictable, although they may have deeply shocked the majority of the population.

The Licentious Monks of St Martin's

A monastery, the priory of St Martin of Tours, occupied the site now taken over by Dover College, close to Dover Priory station. These were farming monks who also offered hospitality to pilgrims travelling from the Continent to the shrine of St Thomas à Becket at Canterbury. In 1295, the monastery was attacked and set on fire by French pirates; everyone fled except for one elderly but courageous monk called Thomas de la Hale. He was swiftly murdered for refusing to divulge where the treasure was concealed. Later, when a move was made to have Thomas de la Hale canonised, the Prior of Canterbury objected because, it is claimed, he was concerned the Dover Thomas might detract from the glory of St Thomas à Becket at Canterbury.

The monastery was dissolved immediately after being visited by King Henry VIII's commissioners in 1535. Most ordinary monasteries were not dissolved until the following year which indicates that something was wrong, since only the most licentious and corrupt of the lesser religious houses were closed with such haste. There was, quite clearly, a two-tier system as far as morality was concerned, since Henry himself was never a worthy role model. The site has been occupied by Dover College since the 1870s.

A Shocking Innovation!

In 1816, an article in *The Times* condemned a new dance fashion – the waltz – frequently practised in Kent's best homes. This dance, says *The Times*, is obscene, a most shocking innovation

Part of the old priory buildings.

where the couples dance closely with their arms wrapped around each other. This simple dance, which can be performed with little or no skill, was actually performed at the Prince Regent's request and was popular with the heir to the throne, Princess Charlotte, and her husband Prince Leopold.

However, the message did not reach the household of the Ransley smugglers, who, although probably not conversant with the precise steps of the waltz, would celebrate their successful enterprises by drinking themselves senseless and dancing naked. These frivolities generally led to loud, drunken orgies. It is claimed, though, that George Ransley took no part in these antics. Surprisingly, this avid pursuer of contraband gin and wine was a teetotaller and remained sober outside the house while his cohorts gleefully indulged their baser instincts.

Poetic Licence

During the eighteenth and nineteenth centuries, only the rich could afford to travel for pleasure and most ordinary people lived and died in or near the place where they were born, with the exception of sailors, soldiers and pilgrims. Until the late nineteenth century, ships often were often unable to enter the harbour at Dover due to its shallowness, and ruthless boatmen exploited passengers by charging them exorbitant fares to row them to their ferry. (The French practised a similar scam at Calais).

When the Dover steam packet was introduced and crossed regularly from Dover to Calais in the 1780s, it proved a great success with the aristocracy who began writing about their travels, describing them as 'Grand Tours'. In the early days, the gentility arrived in Dover on their post-horse or in their post-chaise: then, in 1786, the Royal Mail coach service was implemented, taking only eight hours from London to Dover (providing it did not fall foul of highwaymen and footpads).

Soon the Dover cutters were so highly regarded that they were patronised by bankers, politicians, merchants and lawyers, as well as a love-struck poet! Percy Bysshe Shelley had good reason to be glad of Dover's efficient port. Shelley, one of our greatest poets, was already married when he fell in love with sixteen-year-old Mary Godwin. In 1814, when he was twenty-two, they decided to elope. But first, Shelley invited along Mary's stepsister, Jane (Claire) Clairmont, who was just fifteen. The three of them made for Dover, boarding the first packet they could find. They travelled through France to Switzerland, where Shelley wrote to his wife, Harriet Westbrook, naively suggesting she join them! Instead, in 1816, she threw herself into the Serpentine in London, leaving her unfaithful husband free to marry. (Harriet had also been sixteen when Shelley eloped with her to Scotland in 1811, and he shared her with his friend, T.J. Hogg. His second wife, Mary Shelley, was the author of *Frankenstein*.) The relationship between Percy Shelley, Mary and Jane Clairmont developed into a scandalous *ménage à trois* which continued until Shelley's death in 1822 aged thirty years old.

Drunk in Charge of a Cow!

One of the strangest pub names must be 'The Cause is Altered'. There are several explanations for how the inn acquired its name. One is that the landlord changed his allegiance during the Civil War; another stated it was simply to escape the reputation the inn had of being a den of smugglers. An additional, more appealing allegation was that the pub was adjacent to the Cow Gate in the Old Town where the cowmen passed through and stopped for a drink. When a cowman was asked why he was drunk on duty, he would say, 'The cows is 'alted, so why shouldn't I?' However, no one is sure which explanation is the right one.

The Morning Star Falls from Grace

The *Dover Telegraph* reported on 28 January 1843, that Elizabeth Marsh, who was the landlady of The Morning Star in New Street, was charged with having her house open on Sunday morning last during the hours of Divine Service. Elizabeth Marsh was fined ten shillings and the same in costs.

Mad Drunk!

On Saturday 19 January 1856, the *Dover Telegraph* reported that Catherine Evans had appeared the previous Monday before the mayor and Messrs Elsted, Latham and Cooke charged with being drunk and using obscene language. Police Constable Faith told the court that the previous day, he had seen Catherine Evans in the market place, and the woman was, '... drunk, mad drunk!' while consorting with several soldiers of the British Swiss Legion. Even when she was taken back to the police station, she continued to use obscene language. Catherine Evans was fined ten shillings including costs or seven days in prison in default of payment.

Mr W.P. Eldsted advised Evans to leave the town as soon as her imprisonment had expired before she got into more serious trouble. It was pointed out that Dover, at the present time, was, 'inundated with women of disreputable character, who had been the primary cause of much of the disorderly conduct of soldiers of the British Swiss Legion'.

The Cause is Altered.

Different view of The Cause is Altered (both above by kind permission of The Prince of Wales Sea Training School).

The *Dover Telegraph* suggested that the magistrate was referring to the 'disgraceful proceedings' occurring in the vicinity of New Street, where soldiers were lured into the private homes of females of the most abandoned habits. It was further suggested that the Health of Towns Act should provide for the surveillance of these infamous lodging homes to help Dover strike at the 'root of the evil'.

Priest by Name but not by Nature

On Saturday 2 August 1856, the *Dover Telegraph* reported the case of Olive Augusta Amelia Priest, who appeared before Mr C.B. Wilkins and Mr W. Cooke. Olive Priest came from Southampton, but claimed she was in Dover in search of her brother, a solicitor by the name of Jones. PC Faith charged her with drunkenness, causing an obstruction in Biggin Street and using obscene language when she was taken to the station. Indignantly, Olive denied the charge and said that the police were: '…a parcel of ill-bred, well-fed creatures.' She was fined fourteen shillings and in default of payment, she was committed for fourteen days.

Following this, a further charge of felony was made. When PC Faith had taken her into custody, a jar was discovered on her person. On examination, it was found that it contained three stockings and a night cap, which was claimed to be the property of Mary Brockman, who lived at Queens Court Passage, Biggin Street. Mary Brockman said the property had gone missing from her kitchen and Olive Priest accused Mary of speaking falsely. Olive insisted she could show Brockman her own private mark on the property and said she had bought the jar from a boy because she wanted to keep her sugar in it.

The newspaper report is confusing after this, because it states that Priest was found to be correct in claiming the property was hers. However, she was still committed to a month's hard labour which was to commence after the fourteen days in prison for drunkenness. Possibly there was some other offence leading to this additional punishment omitted from the newspaper report.

The Female Bigamist

On 18 March 1866, Jane Forge married a soldier, Mr John Forge, but their honeymoon was short as John had to leave for India. It is not clear where Jane was living at the time, but shortly after her husband left to fulfil his military duty, Jane moved to Dover. There she met another soldier, Mr Almond Newman, to whom she turned for consolation and subsequently married. But Almond, too, was posted abroad and although he begged Jane to go with him, she refused, which seems to indicate she actually preferred her first choice, John.

In the meantime, first husband John Forge returned and moved in with Jane, but their wedded bliss was interrupted when the truth came out and Jane was summoned to court. Her honesty was compromised when she said she'd believed her first husband, John, was dead, and the prosecution pointed out she'd claimed around £90 of his pay during the period he was abroad. Forge must have been a forgiving type of man, as the two continued to cohabit throughout her trial. Jane Forge was sentenced to one week in prison.

Ill-used by her Own Kind

According to the *Dover Express* of 4 January 1867, a prostitute known as Fanny Stringer, alias Ann Thomsett, was arrested for being drunk and disorderly and for obstructing a footpath. At the Dover police court, PC Bowles said that at twenty to eleven the previous Sunday evening, he'd seen a crowd near the Golden Fleece public house – and there was Fanny, falling about on the pavement. She refused to go away when requested, so PC Bowles had to take her into custody. However, the young prostitute said she had been kicked about by four girls who lived in the house. The landlord, too, had joined in the kicking, and her legs were so badly injured that she could hardly walk. She was imprisoned for three days in default of a small fine and costs, but was first advised to summons the girls who had so ill-used her, although there was no mention in the report of bringing the landlord to court!

Entrance to 'The Grand Shaft'.

The Misappropriation of 'The Grand Shaft'

The Grand Shaft links the town and the barracks on Western Heights and consists of a 140-foot triple staircase, built between 1806 and 1809, meant to provide a shortcut for troops to the harbour in case of invasion. The moats, ditches and forts were mainly used during Napoleonic times when the threat of invasion was most feared. The use of the staircases demonstrates the old class prejudices; one staircase was assigned to 'Officers and their Ladies', another was for 'Sergeants and their Wives' and the third for 'Soldiers and their Women'! Although invasion never came, the shaft was put to regular use by the soldiers to reach the rowdy pubs and seedy brothels in Snargate Street and the pier district.

IX

ROUGH JUSTICE

'My object so sublime / I shall achieve in time / To make the punishment fit the crime'.
(*The Mikado*, Gilbert and Sullivan)

The Wages of Sin

In the 1700s and 1800s, people could be imprisoned for all manner of crimes that seem trivial to our modern-day culture. No doubt there were murderers and highwaymen held in the gaols, but most of the prisoners were unfortunate wretches convicted of comparatively petty crimes, such as vagrancy, absconding from the service of an employer, and so on. As we have already seen in chapter six, sheep-stealing could bring about the death penalty even if the felon had a hungry family to feed.

On the other hand, crimes we would consider very grave indeed were often dismissed. Here are some examples of justice we may not agree with today.

Swift Despatch

During medieval times, Sharpness Cliff in Dover was used for the swift despatch of convicted felons, and was aptly named as The Devil's Drop. (These are the cliffs that overlook Snargate Street). It was customary for the prosecutor to carry out the execution. This is also where the Bredenstone stands and the scant remains of Dover's second Roman lighthouse (Pharos). The ceremony to appoint the new Lord Warden took place here for centuries. Now the new Lord Wardens are appointed at the old priory of St Martins, located in the grounds of Dover College.

An even worse fate than being hurled from a cliff top awaited those convicted at the neighbouring Cinque Port of Sandwich, where thieves were buried alive at Thieves Down.

Between a Rock and a Hard Place!

One housebreaker was executed as a matter of course. William Turmaine was born in 1781 and in 1813, aged forty-two, he was convicted at Dover Town Hall for breaking and entering the house of William Abbott in Margate. Subsequently imprisoned in Dover Town Gaol until the date of his execution, it is not difficult to imagine the terrible fear he must have felt.

Around 11.00 a.m. on 13 March 1813, a cart arrived at the gaol in the market square. Inside it was the Revd Maule, the executioner, the condemned man and his coffin. It is hard to imagine

The Eagle Inn.

how he could have concentrated on the pious words of the reverend. Attending the cart were six constables, two of whom were on horseback. In addition, the cart was followed by many of the local dignitaries and an unruly crowd of locals, all revelling in William's misery. William Turmaine was taken to the high ground on the corner of Tower Hamlets Road and London Road, behind the notorious Black Horse Inn which was auctioned in September 1839, and is now occupied by the Eagle Inn. The original inn, where William Turmaine was taken, had a grisly history, as the land just behind it was Dover's assigned place of execution. It is claimed that the owners of the Black Horse sold tickets to anyone who wanted to watch the executions from the pub.

The Revd Maule said some prayers for the prisoner's soul, and then the executioner came forward with the noose. Some executioners were less compassionate than others, and this one made sure it took William several minutes to die. He was taken to Canterbury to be buried.

Fowl Play

According to *the Dover Telegraph* of the 14 April 1838, a forty-three-year-old man, Peter Runger, was sentenced to be transported for seven years for stealing eighteen fowls at Northbourne.

Vagrants and Beggars

On 28 January 1843, the *Dover Telegraph* reported that Patrick Letty, William Durrant and George Morris were committed to the house of correction for fourteen days for vagrancy, while at Dover police court in 1868, Patrick Kelly, 'a ragged and unknown son of Erin', was charged by Constable Sayers with begging on Admiralty Pier. He was jailed for one week.

A Brutal Murder

On the other hand, sometimes comparatively serious crimes attracted only minor punishment. In the 1840s, Cockering, an Irishman, was staying with his lover, Julia McCarthy, at the Dover Horse and Jockey pub. The landlord heard a terrible struggle upstairs and, on entering the room, found the Irishman had made a brutal attack with a hedge-stake on Julia, who by then was almost unconscious. Although the landlord wanted to call a doctor, Cockering wouldn't allow it and so, Julia McCarthy died. The Irishman was tried for manslaughter in July 1844, but the charge was reduced to one of common assault and Cockering received only a minor punishment.

Accidental Death?

At an inquest in August 1863, held at the Two Brothers public house in Dover, a young boy, Edward Wildish Junior, died through injuries caused by 'accidental scalding.' No blame was placed on his parents and they escaped without punishment.

Anything for a Profit

A baker was summoned to Dover police court on Friday 10 January 1936. George Hayhoe of 140 Buckland Avenue, Dover appeared before Messrs W.J. Barnes and J.W. Bussey. The prosecutor, Mr J.L. Evans, who was the assistant town clerk, told the Bench that the Inspector of Weights and Measures had paid George Hayhoe a visit and found a quantity of loaves for sale which were deficient in weight. None of the loaves weighed one pound, or an integral number of pounds; twenty-six loaves had been weighed, of which twenty were deficient. George Hayhoe pleaded guilty, but as it was a first offence, he got off lightly with a fine of four shillings and costs. This was indeed a light punishment considering that in the early 1900s, there were many people living on or below the 'breadline' with hungry children to feed.

The Worst Kind of Justice

But for the ultimate in rough justice, indeed in any justice at all, the inmates of the workhouse must have the final word. Today, we would see their plight as a crime against humanity, for most were guilty of nothing more sinister than poverty, illness and vagrancy. The Union Workhouse at Buckland Bottom in Dover opened on 29 September 1836, with accommodation for 500 inmates, and was home to those who had lost everything; the unemployed, unmarried mothers, the elderly, the disabled, the sick and the insane. All were expected to perform menial work, perhaps breaking up stones for making roads or chopping wood. Others might apply themselves to oakum-picking, which means teasing out the fibres from used, tarred hemp ropes for sealing the seams of ships, called 'caulking'. This was incredibly painful work.

If anyone dared violate the rules of this punishing regime, perhaps by fighting, quarrelling or causing damage, retribution was immediate and severe, ranging from a whipping to being

The children's block of the Union Workhouse.

deprived of food. Frequently, transgressors were hauled before the magistrate and he would usually send them to prison. Some inmates killed themselves rather than face life in the workhouse. In 1843, George Marsh drowned himself; the next year John Tams cut his own throat, as did William Partridge in 1854. In 1855 Stephen Hicks hanged himself, while Stephen Tolpott hanged himself in 1862. For these men suicide was the only way out, because there was nowhere else to go.

During the First World War, the main workhouse building was redeveloped, but other parts still exist, including the children's workhouse. Here are two individual cases of victims of the workhouse:

John Tams – a pitiful end!

The death of John Tams, mentioned above, was reported in the *Dover Telegraph* on 8 June 1844. At the coroner's inquest, Edward Cresswell, who was a fellow inmate, reported that the previous afternoon, around 5.30 p.m., John was reported missing from the supper table. 'Mr Bentley' sent Edward in search of the missing inmate. He found John Tams in the closet in the old men's yard, still sitting on the seat with the bloody knife in his hand. There was blood all over him and on the floor from a wound in his throat, but he was still alive. John hung on to life for three more hours after being moved to the strong room, but then he died from his wound.

He had become an inmate seven weeks earlier, but because of his 'disordered state of mind' he remained in the infirmary for three weeks. It was revealed that John Tams was full of regret for leaving his work and ruining his family and this had preyed on his mind, leading him to commit this terrible act against himself.

A Pauper's Clothing

William Meredith was an old man whose mind was deranged but, as reported on 22 February 1867 in the *Dover Express*, he was charged at Dover police court with deserting from the Union without handing back his workhouse clothes. William Meredith hardly seemed to understand the nature of his crime in court, and he seemed unaware that he had acted wrongly in keeping the pauper's clothing. In his defence, he said he had arranged for the clothes to be washed and that he intended to send them back.

According to Mr Thurlow, prosecuting, William Meredith was admitted to the Dover Workhouse on 24 November 1866, and remained until 31 December, when he asked for a 'leave of absence' for three days. He left, still wearing the clothes, but he hadn't returned to the Union Workhouse since then. As the clothes were valued at twenty shillings, PC Geddes took the prisoner into custody, although the latter insisted the clothes were at his cousin's house, and this, eventually, was found to be the case. However, as the guardian had instructed Mr Thurlow to prosecute, the magistrate felt he had no option but to commit the poor man to prison for seven days – after all, even if he did not intend to return to the workhouse, he should have returned the clothing.

Kiss and Make Up

At the Dover police court, reported the *Dover Express* of 25 January 1867, John Nolan was charged with beating and generally ill-treating his wife. Immediately, Nolan asked for an adjournment, explaining that his elder son was prevented from attending to give evidence in his father's favour. Nolan was found to be correct in this – his son had been given a shilling not to give evidence against his mother. Apparently, there was also a younger son who sided with the mother.

The couple was encouraged by the magistrate, Sir Luke Smithett, to make things up rather than force their children to give evidence against one or other of their parents, but Mrs Nolan refused to contemplate any reconciliation. Again, Mr Nolan pointed out that his son had been 'bought', and the court erupted into laughter. Then John Nolan requested that he should be allowed to remove his own property from his wife's keeping and this was agreed, although, again, the couple was advised to make up their differences.

It is, of course, impossible today to determine for certain whether or not John Nolan was actually a wife beater – even so, it seems foolhardy to our modern minds that Mrs Nolan should be pressured to make things up without the court first establishing her husband's actual guilt or innocence.

Unequal Rights

At the beginning of the eighteenth century if a woman killed her husband, she was guilty not only of murder, but also of petty treason. This latter crime dated from the Treason Act of 1351 and was brought into force when an 'inferior' committed murder; for example, the killing of a master by a servant, or any superior rank by an inferior rank. This was regarded as a much more serious crime than murder alone. Since women were considered inferior to men, the murder of a husband by his wife was seen as a much graver offence than the reverse. In other words, a crime had been committed not only against the person, but against the state and was perceived as challenging the accepted order. The punishment for petty treason was horrific. Men who committed the crime of petty treason were hanged, drawn and quartered. This latter punishment

Prisoners must have dreamed of escaping into the anonymity of Dover's cliff side.

Impression of a poor woman, 1700s.

was seen as an unseemly punishment for women, as it involved nakedness, so they were burned at the stake for the murder of a husband. The punishment for petty treason was identical to that of high treason.

Between January 1800 and April 1886, it is estimated there were 5,508 public executions in the British Isles and of these, 207 were of women and girls. Until 1836, children were regularly sentenced to death in the British Isles; the youngest appears to have been a boy of seven years, and there is another case of a nine-year-old.

Before The Anatomy Act of 1832 came into force, murderers could be sent for dissection, the contemplation of which, in those superstitious times, was an extra punishment for the victim.

Prisons

Besides the old gaol off Market Square, built around 1740 and breached and destroyed in 1820 (see chapter two), and the prison at the Maison Dieu, which dates from 1834 and runs below and to the side of the building, there was also a military prison which was once under the jurisdiction of the Guston village parish.

Although Guston village is now inland, the parish once extended to the cliffs above Dover Harbour. During 1884, using about a hundred men employed by Denne of Deal, and truckloads of bricks drawn by traction engines and then transported by trolleys on a horse tramway,

Cinque Ports Prison.

Langdon Prison began to take shape on the cliffs. This fell in line with the Government's intention to build an enormous harbour of refuge for the Admiralty of Dover, necessary due to coastal erosion. Before the prison was built, and up until the 1860s, convicts were frequently transported to Australia, but by now Australia had had enough. Once this procedure of dumping our undesirables on that country had ceased, the Government wanted to find ways to usefully employ these convicts, many of whom had only committed trivial offences. To reduce expenses, and because convicts were unwaged, it was decided to use these prisoners for the work, but the plan was never implemented due to the objections of local craftsman who were angry at losing their livelihood. Also, there was a conflict of interests between the Dover Harbour Board and the Government, the former wanting the work completed as quickly as possible, the latter preferring long-term employment for the felons.

Towards the end of August 1885, the first convicts arrived at Dover Priory station, an event reported by the *Dover Express* of 4 September 1885:

> The convicts, fifty in number, were guarded by ten warders, were handcuffed in couples and fastened together in five groups of ten each by chains. They wore the usual convict garb of many colours, red and yellow coats, yellow scotch caps, grey stockings and yellow knickerbockers... They appeared to be a rough, stalwart set of men, the gentlemanly convicts evidently having been reserved for the later arrivals.

The prison closed around 1895 and then reopened in 1901 when it was taken over by the military authorities. Now it was known as Dover Military Prison and was used as such until around 1908, after which it was, again, abandoned. During World War One the prison was used as a barracks, and then partially demolished in 1920. Finally, it was left to fall into decay and the area, now owned by the National Trust and incorporating a terraced car park and picnic area, can be viewed by the public. The former prison is sometimes referred to as Guston Prison because it fell into that parish.

The Cinque Ports Prison was a medieval prison used in the eighteenth and nineteenth centuries specifically for debtors condemned by the Lord Warden's court. It was later used as married quarters for the soldiers. It is located within the grounds of Dover Castle. In the eighteenth century, once it was no longer needed for military use, Peverell's Tower in Dover Castle's grounds became part of the Cinque Ports Prison for a period of time.

Maidstone Prison

From 1831, Maidstone Prison became the place of execution for the entire county of Kent. Then, on 29 Marsh 1868, Parliament passed a bill putting an end to public hangings. A young Dover man, Thomas Wells, became the first person to suffer a private hanging at the prison on 29 March 1868. His case history is documented in chapter twelve.

Whipping – Dover Abhors Inhumane Practice

On 23 November 1844, the *Dover Telegraph* published an indignant piece about a whipping carried out in the town. Apparently, a man had been sentenced in neighbouring Folkestone. Dover was under contract to incarcerate the felon for six months, the sentence to include two public whippings. Dover no longer tolerated such medieval practices but had no authority to interfere with the punishment to be meted out to the unfortunate culprit. Thankfully, however, the second whipping was remitted.

Another view of the Cinque Ports Prison.

The Christmas Vagrant

On a lighter note, it is reassuring to mention that just occasionally the law had a heart in these harsh times of rough justice. According to the *Dover Express* report of 27 December 1867, Mary Davis, a vagrant, was charged with begging on the previous day. The paper described how the Bench was still under the influence of Christmas, and the fortunate Mary Davis was not only dismissed, 'but enriched by a shilling from the pocket of the worthy magistrate.'

X
YOB CULTURE THROUGH THE AGES

I have included 'The Old Woman in the Wall', 'The Stick that Grew' and 'The Drummer Boy at Dover Castle' in this chapter because these stories are fascinating and part of Dover's folklore. However, their historical truth (and the manifestation of the ghost in the case of the latter) cannot, of course, be verified by the usual procedures.

Obnoxious Odo, Bishop of Bayeux

When King William conquered England, his half-brother Odo was Bishop of Bayeux – but that wasn't enough for him. He wanted, someday, to take William's place. His ruthless pursuit of power made him one of the most hated of Dover's historical figures, and his reign of terror spread from Dover across the entire county of Kent.

Odo was greedy to acquire a large fortune in gold and treasure for the longed-for day when he became King, and he set out to destroy all the Saxon landowners and take over their estates. He gave their homes to his friends and family and, in his arrogance, he even confiscated the Guildhall from the King.

In the mid-eleventh century, Dover was a busy port with packet ships leaving regularly for France. This didn't worry Odo; he permitted one of his tenants to build a mill at the entrance to Dover Harbour. This caused such a disturbance to the sea that shipping was affected and many vessels were wrecked as a result.

If all this wasn't enough, around 1082 he decided to ask the English knights to assist him in deposing the Pope so he could take the Papacy for himself. An army was gathered to go to Italy but then Odo was arrested, tried, and condemned under his secular title of the Earl of Kent. He was imprisoned in Normandy until 1087, when he was released by William, who also, generously, restored Odo's earldom. Still the unruly Odo continued his campaign against the new King, William Rufus. After William Rufus attacked Tonbridge Castle, held by Gilbert de Clare, a cohort of Odo's, he then marched on Pevensey Castle, which fell after six weeks due to disease. Here, Odo was captured and sent to Rochester Castle, and the earldom of Kent ceased to exist. So, after thirteen years of terrorizing the county, Odo was exiled; he died in France in 1097.

However, Odo wasn't the only important personage to benefit from the miseries of others during his lifetime. When men were fined for adultery, the King pocketed the cash and also received half the property of those condemned to death. Adulterous women had their fines paid to the archbishop – an ironic justice.

Odo once owned a fine manor house in the village of Coldred. The site is now occupied by Coldred Court Farm.

The Old Woman in the Wall

During the building of Dover Castle, the masons were puzzled by the way Peverell's Tower kept collapsing. They would build it up again and again but still it kept coming down, and no one could work out why. Rather than blame themselves for inadequate workmanship, they decided that evil spirits were about and needed appeasing. They seized an old woman and her dog and interred them in the wall alive, as a sacrifice to the spirits. Vehemently, the terrified old woman cursed them as she and her innocent pet were entombed, but that did not deter the masons. After the building was completed, she had her revenge when the chief mason fell from the top of the tower to his death. It is a fact that people were entombed in buildings to propitiate evil spirits during medieval times, and castles were often alleged to be built on the body of a witch.

The Stick that Grew

A soldier from Dover Castle took a stick and killed another man, but there was no one around to witness the deed. The soldier, whose name was claimed to be Donald in a rather ironic piece

Peverell's Gateway and Tower, Dover Castle.

printed by the *Dover Telegraph* on Saturday 9 Marsh 1844, was convinced he had escaped justice, and in a strange sort of bargain with himself, he pushed the stick into the ground close to the Dover/Deal road, believing he would be safe – so long as the stick did not take root. Later, his regiment was sent abroad, only returning twenty years later. When the soldier arrived at Dover, he discovered, to his astonishment and fear, that the stick had become a fine young elm tree.

Overcome with guilt for what he had done, he confessed, and, as a result, he was tried, found guilty and hanged in chains next to the elm tree. However, the newspaper expressed some reservations about the truth of this story, pointing out that elm trees grow extremely slowly – and that the tree was probably already there.

Sir Thomas Cheyne and Dover Castle

Sir Thomas Cheyne was a noble with his eye on the main chance – and that was Dover Castle.

The defence of the Channel coast was under fierce scrutiny at the end of January 1450. This was due to an incident on Saturday 24 January when plans for a rebellion were hatched in the villages between Dover and Sandwich. The perpetrator of these meetings was Sir Thomas Cheyne. He had a two-pronged plan – to take Dover Castle, and to behead a number of his enemies, among them the Bishop of Salisbury, the Abbot of Gloucester and the Duke of Suffolk. There were a few other matters to attend to, as the rebels planned to rob the priory of Christchurch, Canterbury and other religious buildings. Many of the rebels adopted names to hide their identities, including 'King of the Fairies', 'Queen of the Fairies' and 'Robin Hood', while Cheyne himself was 'The Hermit Blewbeard'(sic).

The following Monday, 26 January, 200 rebels met at Eastry and by the end of the week thousands more had joined them. Cheyne was gathering a hardy band of volunteers to help him in his attack on Dover Castle. But the rebellion only got as far as Canterbury, where

Dover Castle's keep.

St Radigund's Abbey Hospice, located outside the city walls, was attacked. Thomas Cheyne was arrested on 31 January and later hanged, drawn and quartered at Tyburn, while Dover Castle remained unviolated. Cheyne's head was sent to London, and his quarters shared between London, Norwich and two of the ports. No one else was executed as a result of the rebellion.

Bloody Murder in the Castle

A drummer boy who lost his life in Dover Castle is said to be the source of the headless ghost which is claimed to walk the battlements. The boy was on an errand, carrying money for his captain, but he was set upon by thugs. Bravely, he fought his attackers and tried to hang onto the money he was guarding, but he was outnumbered by the ruffians and beheaded. In December, 2002, Living TV's *Most Haunted* programme presented a live show featuring the spirit medium Derek Acorah, some paranormal investigators and an historian. Mr Acorah claimed the attack came from men from the boy's regiment who knew about his errand, and that the boy's headless body was recovered in 1802. Mysteriously, the head was never found. Further details supplied by Mr Acorah claim that the fourteen year-old boy was from Cork in Ireland, and that his mother's name was Mary. He said that he would try to set the boy's spirit free.

An Assault Upon a Hat

In Dover in 1843, a case was brought by a publican against a churchwarden. It appeared the churchwarden took one of his duties rather too seriously, that of ensuring everyone behaved in an orderly, non-yobbish manner in church. When the publican sat in church with his hat still perched on his head, the churchwarden was incensed and whipped it off. The furious publican instigated a civil action for assault, but the case was thrown out.

Dover Castle's battlements.

The One that Got Away!

On 30 November 1844, the *Dover Telegraph* reported the murder of PC Couchman at the hands of a member of the notorious Clark family in the Dover area of Charlton. When people arrived at a public house in Dover, The Three Colts, in anticipation of an open-air prizefight, only to find it had been cancelled due to heavy rain, they had no option but to blot out their disappointment with a drink. John Pine of Dover Police told how he heard a terrible noise, and saw some people quarrelling in the street on Sunday, 8 September. He followed them to Tower Hamlets. Soon around twenty to thirty people, both men and women, were involved in the fight.

When two constables arrived from Dover, even they were intimidated by the affray and sensibly sent for reinforcements; for a start, the troublemakers included a chimney sweep from Canterbury named James Clark, aged sixty, and his strapping sons (variously reported as numbering either four or five), all of whom were prizefighters. Whether or not the sons became more belligerent because of the constables' call for help is unknown, but they decided to take on the policemen.

It is claimed one of the young thugs seized a broom handle and brutally struck at one of the constables. The force of the blow caused the constable to stagger across the floor, finally collapsing. In seconds, he was dead. Unperturbed by the constable's plight, the furious men continued fighting. In due course, James Clark and his scrapping sons were arrested, and appeared in court together with William Smith, aged twenty-three. Ironically, the one who escaped was the cold-hearted killer of the constable.

Two Brothers

A report in the *Deal and Walmer Telegram* relates how Thomas and Henry Redsull were enjoying themselves having a brotherly drink in the North End in Middle Street, Deal, late one Tuesday night in October 1863. They were challenged to a fight by another man and ended up in court on 10 October 1863, charged with being drunk and riotous. They explained that they had been working in their boats all day and needed some beer before they went to bed. They each had to pay a fine of eight shillings for their disorderly conduct.

The Two Brothers opened in 1851, but the renewal of its licence was refused in 1869. It re-opened for a short time, but the licence was refused again in 1870, presumably due to customers like the brothers Redsull!

Furious Driving!

According to the *Dover Express* dated 4 January 1867, William Marsh, a meat contractor to the forces, was charged with driving furiously. A sergeant, Isaac Redman of the 44th Regiment, told the court that on the evening of the 24 December 1866, at 5.00 p.m., he was walking along Snargate Street on the kerb when he heard someone driving furiously. Before he could look around, he was knocked down and the wheel of the cart driven by William Marsh went over a part of his body (the report does not say which part was run over). Then Patrick Thomas Flanaghan, a private, said he was in the cart driven by Marsh, as he had been sent from the barracks to obtain meat, and he duly cautioned the meat contractor. The magistrate stated that he was determined to put a stop to 'furious driving', and fined the defendant ten shillings and ten shillings costs.

I won't pay nothing!

A case was tried against a soldier at Dover police court in 1868. A fruit dealer named William Hopper, who lived in New Street, kept a stall in the market place for the sale of fruit and other commodities. He was going about his business at around 8.30 p.m. when a soldier of the Royal Artillery approached and, with no apparent motive, seized his fruit stall at the bottom and overturned it. Apples, gingerbread and bulls' eyes were flung everywhere. Angrily William Hopper challenged the soldier: 'Hallo Guv'nor, what are you about?' At this, the soldier threatened William Hopper with his fists, hit him on the face, and then ran away.

PC Barton was on duty in the neighbourhood of the market place and, at around 9.00 p.m. that evening, he learned of the artillery man's attack on Hopper and his stall. At the scene of the crime, he noted fruit, peppermints and glass all over the pavement, and interviewed witnesses who informed him the soldier had run off up Biggin Street. William Hopper requested that the soldier be taken into custody, so Constable Barton set off in pursuit. He found the soldier, one John Humphreys, and ordered him to accompany him to the police station. John Humphreys replied, 'No six policemen in the force can make me go against my will.' Then he struck PC Barton in the mouth.

In court, Hopper, still amazed at this unprovoked and malicious attack on him and his property, charged John Humphreys with assault and with maliciously inflicting damage on his goods when he overturned the stall. Hopper claimed his losses amounted to around five shillings, but he would forgo the charge if the defendant paid for the damage he had caused. However, the prisoner remained surly and replied, 'I won't pay nothing'. When the magistrate asked Humphreys to explain himself, he said that Hopper had called him a '....... soldier!' as he passed by, although this was strongly disputed by the complainant.

The magistrate believed William Hopper, and fined Humphreys the amount of five shillings as well as costs in default of paying, but on the soldier's refusal to co-operate, he was committed to prison for one week. It was also agreed that Humphreys should be convicted of the second charge of attacking the police officer. However, in mitigation, the prisoner's general character was good when sober, although he became violent under the influence of drink. Again, the magistrate set the fine at five shillings and costs, but in default, Humphreys would have to spend an extra week in prison. 'I would rather go to prison for six weeks than pay a farthing', said John Humphreys (a farthing was a quarter of a penny in imperial money). The magistrate had no choice but to commit the defiant soldier to prison to reflect upon his nasty temper.

The Christmas Hanging

Alfred Lawrence was thirty-two years old and his girlfriend, Violet Hubbard, was forty-seven. During the summer of 1912, Alfred Lawrence battered Violet at a house in Portland Place, Dover, and then he cut her throat. He was tried for murder by Justice Channel in late November 1912, and the jury at Maidstone pronounced him guilty. He was sentenced to death, and was hanged a few days before Christmas by the executioner, John Ellis.

XI

TWO TRAGIC SISTERS
AND A SOLDIER

On Saturday 9 August 1856, The *Dover Telegraph* reported a horrific murder committed the previous Sunday, stating that: '…within four or five miles of the town lay the murdered corpses of two young females, who, accompanied by a soldier of the British Swiss Legion, had left their homes early in the morning to spend the day at Shorncliffe encampment.'

The two young sisters from Dover, Caroline, aged eighteen, and Maria Back, aged sixteen, met their deaths at the hands of a twenty-five-year-old soldier from Belgrade, Dedea Redanies. Caroline had lived with her parents at Albion Place and her younger sister Maria was in service to a tradesman in Snargate Street. Dedea Redanies was first suspected of the crime when he failed to return to return to the camp at the expected time.

Redanies, the son of a civil servant, was serving with the 2nd Battalion of the British Swiss Legion and was a Moslem by birth, but had been converted to Christianity by a monk in Milan. Able to speak German, Italian and some English, he was employed as an interpreter at Dover Castle and was also responsible for carrying regimental laundry to Dover.

There are some inconsistencies about how Redanies met Caroline; outside a Dover Theatre, as claimed in one report, or at the house of her mother, Mrs Back, who took in washing for soldiers at the family's home in Albion Place, in another. Either way, when he met the pretty young woman, he couldn't believe his luck.

He courted Caroline but began to suspect that she did not feel as strongly for him as he felt for her, although when he saw an artillery man in the house, he did not suspect anything at first. Posted to Aldershot for a period, he continued to write to Caroline and, on returning, wanted to see the letters he'd sent her. She brought them to him readily enough, unaware that there was a letter from the sergeant from Woolwich in the batch. Redanies didn't get a chance to read it properly before Caroline noticed, pounced on it and flung it in the fire. But he'd seen enough and he became consumed by jealousy.

Their relationship deteriorated when on Saturday, 2 August 1856, Caroline informed her lover that she wanted to stay with her sister in Woolwich for a time. She handed Redanies a miniature portrait of himself that he'd given her, as she had no further use for it. Furiously, Redanies smashed the picture, although he later relented and promised to get her a larger one. That evening, around 6.00 p.m., Redanies visited the shop of cutler John Green and purchased a kind of flick knife called a 'poignard'. Arriving back at Albion Place around 7.30 p.m., he told Caroline he wanted to take their relationship a step further by introducing her to his sister, who

The footpath along the cliff top.

was visiting the camp. (This was later described by the court as a 'specious plea'). In any case, Mrs Back had other ideas; for one thing, Caroline was not well enough to make the journey so late, and especially not unchaperoned. However, she would allow her daughter to accompany Redanies to Shornecliffe Barracks the following morning, providing younger sister Maria accompanied them.

The following morning, the sisters got up around 2.00 a.m. and ate breakfast with their father, John Back, at 2.30 a.m. Then, at 3.00 a.m. on 3 August, the three young people set off to walk to the camp, but little did the sisters realize that Redanies was carrying a knife. By about 5.00 a.m., they had almost reached Dover, but stopped short at Capel le Ferne where the Valiant Sailor stood near to a place called Steddy Hole. There, in Steddy Hole, a hollow in a secluded spot not far from the Folkestone Old Turnpike, Redanies stabbed sixteen year-old younger sister Maria four times around the heart; then he set about his girlfriend, Caroline, also stabbing her around the heart. The girls were not seen again until the bodies were discovered about 8.00 a.m. the following morning. They were about sixteen paces apart and forty feet from the edge of the cliff.

Thomas Gurling, who had discovered the bodies, hurried to tell the landlord of The Valiant Sailor, Richard Kitham, that a murder had taken place nearby. The two men went to find the bodies, which were taken to a nearby house and later identified by their distraught mother. It was later reported that Maria seemed to have died without a struggle, and of the four stab wounds to her heart area, three had pierced the lungs and any of these could have been fatal. Her elder sister Caroline had struggled hard and had also sustained four stab wounds, but, in addition, her fingers were lacerated as though she had grasped at the weapon used to attack her.

Meanwhile, Redanies, having left their bodies where they lay, tried to escape to Canterbury, and was spotted on the Folkestone Road by PC Herd, who recognized him from a previous occasion when Redanies had fallen foul of the law. Early Monday morning, he was woken up by some boys at Black Robin Corner near Capel le Ferne. He bought himself some bread and cheese for sixpence. Redanies stopped at Lower Hardres to buy pen, paper and envelopes from a grocery shop run by Mrs Elizabeth Atwood. The date was Monday 4 August, and he wrote in German to his commanding officer, Lieutenant Schmidt, as well as to Mrs Back begging forgiveness for murdering her young daughters. After posting both letters in Lower Hardres, nothing was seen of the runaway from noon until 3.00 p.m., when he was spotted by a man who said, 'Here comes the fellow.'

Redanies saw that he had caught the attention of the watching men and in the violent struggle that followed, he stabbed himself three times in the breast. A Constable Foyer had attended the scene. Redanies was taken to Canterbury Hospital where he confirmed that he had, 'done something dreadful.' Strangely, he was carrying the two little black capes worn by the girls, and on being admitted to hospital, another article of girl's clothing was found on his person. Later, it emerged that he had taken the black capes to wear as his 'mourning suit'. He was bleeding so badly on arrival at Canterbury Hospital that it was feared he might not live. The knife with which he had stabbed himself was nine inches long and one inch in breadth, and

Steddy Hole, now spelled 'Steady Hole'.

The Valiant Sailor today (April 2006). The pub is now closed and empty of furnishings.

it had penetrated six inches deep into his lungs. The following Tuesday night, he requested the knife be brought to him so he could 'finish himself off'.

At his trial, Dedea Redanies needed his own interpreter, but he seemed to remain unaffected by the proceedings. He pleaded guilty to Caroline's murder, but not to Maria's. Redanies simply said, 'Maria got in the way.' Although he claimed to have had a serious argument with Caroline, there was no witness to support this, nor was his claim that Caroline had been deceiving him with Sergeant Tiffin from Woolwich accepted in mitigation. In any case, his defence was seriously compromised when the cutler came forward to account for the purchase of the knife, while the self-inflicted wounds on Redanies' own body matched exactly those on Maria's. This was a murder that was clearly premeditated and, as such, it was 'wilful murder'; therefore, Dedea Redanies was duly pronounced guilty.

This was to be the first execution in seven years at Maidstone, but before Redanies went to the scaffold, it is claimed Mrs Back came to visit him and forgave him. Throughout his confinement, Dedea Redanies was convinced that all he had done was to send the two girls to heaven before him, and that soon they would all be reunited. On the day of his execution, New Year's Day 1857, at 8.45 a.m., Redanies went to the chapel to get ready to meet the infamous Calcraft, and then his God. The *Dover Telegraph* reported that Dedea Redanies went to his death on Thursday 1 January at noon in front of the county gaol at Maidstone. The paper remarked on his perfect composure and impassivity, and maybe this was because he had been well prepared.

The Revd King was the chaplain at the gaol, and he realized that Dedanies needed spiritual consolation from a Roman Catholic source, so a priest named Father Lawrence was found who also had a knowledge of German. Father Lawrence administered the sacrament to Redanies on the Wednesday before the execution, although at one stage the Roman Catholic priest said he believed the prisoner was insane. (Although a letter had been written to the Secretary of State, no reprieve had been granted.) The authorities permitted Redanies five indulgencies, one of which was to smoke his pipe just before he died.

Approaching his death with indifference, he is reported as saying: 'In a few moments I shall be in the arms of my dear Caroline – I care not for death.' He held himself in an upright military manner as he walked to the gallows and climbed the steps, submitting to the pinioning without resistance. The Revd King read the burial service in English and then Father Lawrence read prayers in German.

He was put to death in front of a gathering of 5,000 people. Today we would call them 'rubbernecks' or worse, but, although in those times a hanging was sometimes an excuse for a good day's sport, it was reported that the gathering was orderly and respectful. The scaffold stood on top of the porter's lodge of the prison, so it seemed everyone had a clear view. When the drop fell, Dedea Redanies died instantaneously.

The letter Redanies wrote to the girls' mother began 'Dear Mother Back.' He told her he preferred Caroline to die rather than belong to another, and that he did not intend to murder Maria, but she was in his way. He told Mrs Back that he had asked the girls to sit down in the hollow, but they refused because the grass was wet. When he stabbed Caroline, she cried out, 'Dear Dedea', and then she fell down with weeping eyes. 'Then I rushed over to her and gave her the last kisses as an everlasting remembrance…my broken heart could not tell where my senses had gone.'

An extra tragic footnote to this story appeared at the bottom of the column under the heading: 'Fatal Accident After the Execution'. When two men began to dismantle the gallows, one of the heavy crossbeams came away unexpectedly, so that one of the labourers fell to the ground, a drop of around fifteen feet, and died.

XII

THE SHOOTING AT DOVER PRIORY STATION

The murder victim was Edward Walshe, an employee of the London, Chatham and Dover Railway and a station master at Dover Priory railway station in the 1860s. News of his brutal murder first appeared in the *Dover Express* on 1 May 1868 under the heading: 'Shocking Tragedy at Dover', and continued: 'Just as we go to press, the town of Dover is startled by an occurrence as very rarely takes place in this quiet community, viz. the crime of murder.' The paper described Wells as 'the assassin', a man of a morose disposition and the son of a fishmonger in Round Tower Street. The weapon Wells used on Mr Walshe belonged to his father. The character of Mr Walshe was held to be: 'superior and intelligent…he was called to the bar in the early part of his career.'

On Friday, 8 May 1968, the paper reported that the coroner's inquest, held at 1.00 p.m. the previous Saturday, had found that Wells had shot the stationmaster through the front of the head so that his skull was shattered. The court procedures moved extremely fast, as this was a clear-cut case with strong witnesses, and so the court was adjourned till the following Tuesday. The coroner, Mr V.H. Payn, stated that this adjournment would only be a formal proceeding, and so it was, with the verdict duly signed and the warrant issued.

It was decided that: 'Stationmaster Edward Adolphus Walshe died from the effects of a gun shot wound, wilfully inflicted by Thomas Wells.' (The main witnesses were Mr Henry Cox, superintendent at the station, A.G. Osborne, surgeon, and John Golder, a porter.) Edward Walshe, who was said to be a disciplinarian, was dissatisfied with his young employee Thomas Wells, aged eighteen, whose work as a porter and cleaner was slipshod. He was also disobedient and had to be admonished for taking his gun to work and firing at birds instead of applying himself to the carriage-cleaning for which he was employed. Thomas Wells was incensed one day when he was ordered by Edward Walshe to cart a quantity of manure to the man's own garden, and that was what motivated him to bring the gun to work. On 29 April 1868, he had to be cautioned for using the gun at the station for target practice, and was overheard saying 'I'll let the old 'b' have it!'

One of Thomas Wells' regular duties was to board an evening train destined for Harbour station where he had to clean out the carriages. That evening, he boarded the brake van, then changed his mind at the last moment and leapt off the moving train before it left the station, causing more aggravation with his boss.

At 6.30 a.m. the following day, 30 April, Thomas Wells was summoned to Walshe's office, and he must have guessed why as he'd been issued with warnings before, but, in his opinion, his work was up to standard and he thought Edward Walshe was picking on him. Mr Walshe asked him what he had done with the gun and Thomas Wells replied that he had thrown it away. Edward Walshe gave him two options – apologise and promise not to repeat his behaviour or be dismissed. Thomas had ten minutes to think about it. After that reprimand, Thomas Wells became angry enough to get his gun, which he had hidden somewhere in the station. As he entered the office a few minutes later, Edward Walshe was talking about Thomas to his superior, Mr Henry Cox, superintendent at the station.

Thomas raised the gun and shot Edward Walshe point-blank through the head. The ball entered the front of his head, and exited the back, shattering his skull. Then, in a panic, Wells fled from the office and found somewhere to hide. It did not take long for the police to find him crouching in an empty carriage, and he was arrested for the murder of Edward Walshe by Superintendent Coram and Police Sergeant George Stevens.

His trial took place at Kent Summer Assizes at Maidstone. His defence counsel pleaded insanity, which he attributed to an accident at the station when Thomas was almost crushed by a train, having got between a carriage and an engine, one of which rolled and trapped him between the buffers. Semi-conscious, with head and chest injuries, he had suffered badly and this, his parents claimed, had made him aggressive. However, Mr Justice Wills rejected the plea. In those days, the comparative youth or misfortune of a criminal was not allowed to pervert the accepted course of justice, judicial hanging, and Thomas was convicted of wilful murder and sentenced to death.

After sentencing he was taken to a police cell for the condemned, and on the way from the court to the police station, he nodded to people he recognised among the crowd. At the police station, he was able to see his brother, two of his sisters and his sweetheart, and these interviews were later described as 'painful.' His mother became hysterical and remained critical for some time.

Thomas Wells wrote around one hundred letters to people from whom he sought forgiveness, including Henry Cox and Mrs Walshe, the station-master's widow. He spent much time in prayer with the chaplain, the Revd Frazer.

On 29th May 1868, Parliament had passed a bill, the Capital Punishment within the Prisons Bill, which put an end to public hangings. Thus, Thomas became the victim of the first private hanging in Britain, which took place at Maidstone Prison on 13 August 1868 in the prison timber yard, once used as an exercise yard for the prisoners. On Friday 14 August 1868, the *Dover Express* described the apparatus of punishment in detail in their report of the execution:

> The drop is on a perfect level with the stone paving of the yard and the executioner has to descend several stone steps to remove the bolt which supports the platform. The latter then drops into a recess prepared for it. The apparatus is a permanent fixture screened from sight when not in use by moveable shutters.

In fact, outside of the prison wall, the only sign that a hanging was about to take place was the hoisting of a black flag.

Although it was described as the first private hanging to be carried out in England, in attendance were the governor, surgeon, chaplain and sixteen journalists eager to describe the gory details of the death for their readers. Also, the gallows had been used before for public hangings. The execution took place at 10.30 a.m. and two warders supported Thomas Wells as he stood on the trapdoor. The executioner was the dreaded William Calcraft, who specialised in ensuring his victims a slow and painful death by using a short rope, and he was assisted by George Smith of Dudley. Young Thomas Wells went to his death singing a hymn in a loud voice. He died after two or three convulsive struggles against the noose and the pinioning straps; this is

Above: *Dover Priory Station, 1876 (by kind permission of www. dover-kent.co.uk).*

Left: *Dover Priory Station today.*

reported as having taken just under four minutes. After he was cut down around 9.00 p.m. his remains were saved for his own inquest, since a new act of Parliament now required this formality for anyone dying at the hands of the law. Between 1868 and 1899, around a dozen young people between seventeen and nineteen years were hanged.

XIII

IN SEARCH OF WEALTH
AND POWER

In 1896, Arthur Burr founded the first Kent coal company and continued to run it for nearly twenty years. He began by drilling into Shakespeare Cliff in Dover at an estimated cost of £50,000, with the aim of producing 3,000 tons of coal a day by the year 1900. The colliery cost over a million pounds and did not succeed in producing coal commercially. This is particularly ironic since work had already taken place with a view to excavating a Channel tunnel under the authority of Sir Edward Watkins. This project was abandoned by 1890, as it was considered that mining for coal would be a more valuable undertaking than a cross-Channel link.

To be fair to Burr, there were obstacles; for example, the coal was buried deep and was of poor quality. Additionally, there was the constant threat of flooding, and this occurred three times before work had reached halfway down the coal seam. An attempt to make the seam safer by shoring it up with steel rings did not solve the problems. The *Dover Express* reported an incident in 1893 when a father of five, Henry Fisher from Dover, died when he disregarded the threat of 'fire damp', otherwise known as methane gas. Henry Fisher stopped to retrieve his hat, a fatal mistake. Tragically, another man, Charles Horton, tried to assist his workmate and he was also killed. The following year, a sudden surge of water killed eight more men. Then, in March 1896, the Kent Coalfield Syndicate Ltd took over the rights to the Shakespeare Colliery.

Arthur Burr was undeterred; he started several other collieries but still he encountered the same problems, and none of these enterprises produced coal commercially until 1912. The truth was that it was cheaper to employ experienced boring teams from the Continent rather than to bring in men from other British coalfields. This did not stop Burr from producing highly optimistic forecasts to shareholders who were drawn in by promises of quick gains and parted readily with their money as soon as a new project was initiated.

Burr constantly teetered on the brink of bankruptcy. Work frequently came to a halt for a lack of money, although he tried to compensate by purchasing second-hand machinery for the collieries at Tilmanstone and Snowdown. Then, in 1912, there was great excitement as coal was brought up from Snowdown Colliery. It must have been a great moment when in 1913, Arthur Burr, who was much admired by Sir Arthur Conan Doyle, was described as a great benefactor and given the freedom of Dover.

By 1917, Tilmanstone Colliery had begun to show a profit, but it was too late. The years of economic instability could not be overcome that easily. One can imagine the frustration of a driven man, how Arthur Burr was tempted to mislead the shareholders and how, like a gambler, he wanted to believe that his bold plans would one day make him rich. To overcome his financial difficulties, Burr formed a number of companies. Each would own a part of the enterprise; mineral rights, shaft digging, the erection of buildings at the surface, etc. In this way he made sure that money moved around and he was able to show profits. If one company was struggling, it would simply borrow funds from another; today we might call it 'creative accounting'. In 1910, he already owned a colossal twenty-two companies.

Of course, the shareholders reacted badly to this situation, since they received only nominal profits for their investments. In 1914, everything came to a head and Arthur Burr had no option but to resign from his many companies. He was bombarded on all sides by legal actions for the fraudulent misuse of the funds, and it is claimed the shortfall was in the region of £80,000. At his trial, the judge stated that Burr was a dangerous rogue and he was declared bankrupt, dying shortly afterwards in 1919 with many of his debts still unpaid.

A sad footnote is this: today, it is claimed that around 3,000 million tons of coal lay beneath the county of Kent. The story of Arthur Burr is full of such ironies.

XIV

THE DOUBLE MURDER
AT SNARGATE STREET

On Friday, 20 March 1936, a report appeared in the *Dover Express* about the double murder of two babies discovered in a trunk at Snargate Street:

> A sensation was caused in Dover on Friday [13 March 1936] when twin babies of 5 months were found dead in a trunk in Snargate Street. Later a charge of murder was made against the mother, and on Saturday she appeared before magistrates when a remand was ordered till Thursday, on which day a further remand was made. The inquest was opened on Tuesday and adjourned.

At the inquest on the death of the two children, the coroner said that since the cases were identical, they should be treated as one.

Over the next few weeks the tragic story unfolded. Gladys Amelia Varley first appeared in court on the Saturday morning before the mayor, Alderman G.M. Norman, to be charged with the children's murder. She was placed on remand for eight days, in order to make arrangements for her to be properly represented through legal aid. At her next court appearance, where she was represented by Mr J.H. Mowll, with Mr J.L. Evan prosecuting, she was charged that she did feloniously, wilfully and with malice aforethought kill and murder her two children, Peter Varley and David Varley, aged five months, between the dates of 28 February 1936 and 13 March 1936. The case was further remanded till Thursday 26 March.

During a subsequent court appearances, the court heard more of the tragic story. Gladys Varley was actually the mother of five children, although the eldest two, aged five and nine, were living in a Barnardo's Children's Home. This left a young daughter, Joyce, who was aged around two years when the boy twins were born on 28 September 1935 at the Dover Poor Law Institution. At first the little boys were named David and Peter, but after her discharge from the institution on 8 October, Gladys Varley changed their names to William and Brian.

The accused was married to her first husband at seventeen-and-a-half on the 2 October 1927, but in 1932 he left her with no support or income and was now held in prison on a 'bastardy' charge, with a further two similar charges against him. At almost twenty-three-years-old in October 1932, Gladys Varley, with no means of support, was forced to apply for poor relief. Her second husband, the father of Joyce and the twins, was a serving member of the RAF and had also abandoned her before the babies were born, nor did he pay any money for the upkeep of his family.

No. 149 Snargate Street is no longer here, although Number 148 still exists. The boys' bodies were discovered where the boarded-up hotel stands, just beyond the lamp-post.

A witness, Mrs Winifred Barringer, wife of Ernest Barringer, who lived in a house at No. 2 Elizabeth Street (Gladys Varley's previous address), said she had first seen the little boys at eleven days old. Winifred often helped out, taking care of the boys, first the smallest one, then later, when Gladys found work, Winifred took them both and knew them as William and Brian. She confirmed that she had looked after the twins until 29 February, and had then returned them to their mother when Gladys found rooms at No. 149 Snargate Street. A jurist enquired whether the twins were returned at the mother's request and Winifred said that was not the case. When pressed about why they were returned, Winifred claimed she was reluctant to part with them but she had to. While the two women had lived in the same house, Winifred had looked after them, but now Gladys Varley had rooms elsewhere. What had worried Winifred was that she had not seen the little boys since Gladys Varley and her children had left.

The jury were told that a post-mortem was conducted on Peter by J.R.W. Richardson, police surgeon, on 13 March. It was found that he had died more than a week ago, but certainly no longer than a fortnight. Death was due to asphyxia brought on by strangulation from a cord tightened around his neck. David's death was identical. They weighed only 8lb 8oz and 6lb 3.5oz respectively.

Gladys Varley appeared again on the 3 April 1936 before the mayor, Mr G.M. Norman, charged with the murder of her babies, with Mr H.J. Parham prosecuting, Mr Hopkinson defending, and Mr E.E. Chitty representing the NSPCC. It was alleged that on the 13 March the children were found dead in a suitcase labelled with an address, partly obliterated, which indicated No. 129 Radigund Road, the address of the accused's parents. The suitcase was hidden behind a door of an outhouse at No. 149 Snargate Street, where Gladys Varley and her little daughter had lived since leaving Mrs Wilson's property at No. 2 Elizabeth Street (where Mrs Barringer had also lived).

Inspector Fletcher of the NSPCC described how he had tried to convince Gladys Varley she should go to the poor law institution, but Gladys was defiant and said she couldn't bear the thought of being locked up. Friends and neighbours gave their evidence of events leading up to the horrific discovery. Once Gladys left for Snargate Street, they were alarmed to find that the twins were never with their mother, who always made excuses, saying they were asleep or having their bottles, or sometimes being minded by someone else. On the Saturday after Gladys Varley's departure, Mr Wilson, husband of the landlady of the house at No. 2 Elizabeth Street, asked about the twins and was told they had been taken away. Mrs Winifred Barringer had seen Gladys Varley several times since she had vacated the house and the young mother always told her the twins were all right.

One day Gladys Varley managed to prevent Mrs Barringer from entering her house by saying that 'Jim' was lying down. This was alleged to be Jim Watson, a soldier of the Royal Scots, who was, presumably, Gladys' boyfriend. On Tuesday 3 March, Mrs Barringer went to the house again, asking to see the twins. She said: 'If you have done anything to them or there is anything the matter with them, you will get your knuckles rapped and rapped sore.' To this Gladys replied: 'What the …do you take me for? I may be a rogue but not a murderer'.

On Friday 6 March, Winifred Barringer went to Snargate Street when Gladys Varley was out. Winifred told Mrs Nicholls she was worried and so the two women had a look around, and found the pram in the wash-house. Then, on Sunday 8 March, Gladys Varley came to Winifred's lodgings to tell her that a Mrs Hobman and her assistant had now taken the twins. Mrs Frances

Elizabeth Street sign. Today, due to modernisation, most of the old Elizabeth Street has been lost.

Gladys Varley may have been forced to work in a laundry like this one at the old Union Workhouse, Buckland Bottom.

Ida Nicholls, who lived at Snargate Street with her daughter, Kitty, confirmed Glady Varley came to her for a room. The young mother gave her name as Gladys Revell, saying she had one child, and she subsequently took the room at seven shillings per week. She told Mrs Nicholls that her husband was in the Royal Scots and had a 'sleeping out' place. The following day, Gladys Varley arrived with the trunk. At this time, Mrs Nicholls was busy giving music lessons to three pupils, but remembered she did not see the twins in the pram, and her thirteen-year-old daughter confirmed this.

Mr Fletcher, the NSPCC inspector who had already placed the older children in a home, also described visits to Snargate Street where he had talked to Gladys Varley. She had insisted she could not bear to be locked up, because she was a young person and her future was not in an institution for life. She insisted a man called Mr McPhee had agreed to pay her rent. Again, the inspector said that he had not seen the twins when he visited.

Charles Edward Ratcliffe of No. 146 Folkestone Road was the Relieving Officer for Kent County Council at Dover. Gladys Varley had first come to his notice on the 20 July the previous year, and he awarded her temporary relief. On 25 January 1936 he denied her further relief and instead suggested she entered an institution. As a result of this, Mr Faver, Ratcliffe's assistant, gave her an order for herself and the three children to go into the institution, but she refused to comply, saying a man would pay for her rooms. She was afraid of being sent to the workhouse in Lincolnshire, her husband's home county, far away from all her friends and relatives.

On 13 March at 11.45 a.m., Gladys Varley was interviewed by police about another matter. The chief constable asked her how many children she had and she replied that there were five, two of whom were in a Barnardo's home and Joyce at Mrs Wilson's. When the Chief Constable asked her about the twins, she replied: 'I want to make a clean breast of it.' She was cautioned and then she made her statement.

'I had no money to feed them with. The relief people refused to give me any. Joyce was all right. Mrs Wilson gave her some food, but the other two, they died. They are still at

Mrs Nicholls' [the landlady at Snargate Street]. They died a week ago on Monday last. They are in my room at Mrs Nicholls' house lying on my bed.'

A police search by DS Datlen and PC J.G. Moore on Friday 13 March at resulted in the gruesome discovery of the babies in the suitcase. They were covered with pillows and sacks, but it was possible to see the heads of the two babies through the broken end of the suitcase. When charged, Gladys Varley stated she would not say anything, preferring to wait until the court appearance.

A photographer, Arthur Henry Whorwell from Bench Street, recorded the death scene at Snargate Street, attended by Datlen (in some reports, Detective Sergeant Datlen is referred to as Inspector Datlen). Later, the mortuary confirmed the details regarding the indented flesh and obstruction of the respiratory passages, adding that the children were very poorly nourished, a fact confirmed by the contents of their stomachs. Mrs Winifred Barringer said the little boys were in the same clothes as the morning she'd dressed them herself. It was claimed the cord around David's neck came from his woollen leggingettes.

The trial took place at the central criminal court of the Old Bailey, London, on Thursday 23 April, where Gladys Varley's defending counsel, Mr F.A. Hopkinson, pleaded not guilty to the charges on her behalf. Mr B.H. Waddy was also assigned to the defence, while Mr Eustace Fulton and the Hon. Quentin Hogg attended for the prosecution. The *Dover Express* noted that there were three women on the jury but one was challenged by the defending counsel Mr Waddy because she was deaf, and she was replaced by a male juror.

Various pleas were made; for instance, DS Datlen confirmed that when he examined the rooms, there was no food apart from one small piece of bread and two empty milk bottles. Also, the accused came from a disturbed background, since her grandfather committed suicide by hanging himself in 1904, and then her uncle killed himself in 1920 by the same method. Sometimes Mr Hopkinson's defence seemed to clutch at the flimsiest of possibilities; for example, he suggested that despite the tight cords and ribbons, the twins might have died through an accident, for example, suffocation, and that the cords were not necessarily placed around their necks while they were still alive. Perhaps Mr Hopkinson had some compassion for the plight of a desperate young mother who had no food to give her babies, but still could not bear to sacrifice her freedom to life in an institution.

Mr Waddy, too, pleaded for mercy to be shown, pointing out that with a total relief of only nine, and then fifteen shillings to support five children, it was inevitable she should turn to a young soldier for help. The judge agreed that it was a painful case, but there was no insanity involved that could be used in her favour. The jury retired for only about nine minutes, with a verdict of guilty but a recommendation for mercy.

It was concluded that Gladys Varley had murdered her children by asphyxia, and had placed them in the suitcase. Gladys Varley was found guilty of wilful murder and sentenced to death.

The Law

The Infanticide Act of 1922 had reduced the killing of a newborn baby by its mother to a non-capital offence. In 1938, two years after the sad case of Gladys Varley and her twins, the 1922 bill was amended to remove the death penalty against women who killed their babies in the first year of life.

XV

TROUBLE WITH THE NEIGHBOURS

There are always certain people in the neighbourhood who make other people's lives a misery, apparently out of sheer awkwardness, envy, lack of consideration or just the desire for a quick profit. Here are a few nineteenth and twentieth century examples:

Ladies Who Lunch!

On 6 May 1843, the *Dover Telegraph* reported a fracas between some well-to-do ladies from the posh end of town, who, in the reporter's opinion, should have known better.

Mrs Mary Rogers appeared to defend herself against a complaint by Mrs Ann Towson, who said Mrs Rogers had beaten and ill-treated her. The newspaper made much of the fact that these ladies hailed from the 'aristocratic' region of Mount Pleasant, and the journalist took every opportunity to ridicule them for their upper-class accents, describing how the complainant opened her case with 'true blarney'.

Ann Towson told their worships that she had visited a friend's house upon a 'leetle money transaction', and how a busybody, Mrs Mary Rogers, had listened at the window to find out what they were saying. As everyone knew, Ann Towson declared, listeners never heard any good of themselves. Apparently, Mary Rogers was furious at what she heard and broke the window with her hand and then set about assaulting Ann Towson and calling her hard names. Further, she had called her unmentionable things, which she as a respectable married female '…could not think of repating to sich rispictable gentlemen (sic).' The defendant had then pitched into the complainant, and according to the paper, '…very grievously damaged her illigant person.' Clearly, the reporter enjoyed making fun of the ladies' upper-class accents.

Subsequently, four female witnesses came forward to prove the case, and then another four to disprove it. It was '…a regular Irish Babel and a precious scene ensued,' says the paper, and their worships were unable to re-establish order among the elegant ladies for some time. Mrs Rogers was fined one shilling and costs, a total of twelve shillings, to pay within seven days – or, in default, she would spend the same period in the interior of the gaol.

The Rat-Catcher

Not all rat-catchers were forced to exterminate their quarry immediately. On the contrary, if they put them into a sack alive and took them to the local inn to be thrown to the dogs in the rat pit, the sport would entertain the riotous crowd and the dirty work could be done for a generous reward.

Mr J. Watson, a resident of Princes Street, attended Dover Local Board of Health Managing Committee in 1859, presided over by the mayor of Dover and Councillors Back, Dickeson, Walter, Rutter, Stockwell, Clark and Terry.

Mr Watson explained his feud with his unsavoury neighbour, Jacob Pother, a rat-catcher by profession. Jacob Pother lived in considerable filth and kept some very unpleasant terrier dogs who barked constantly. The dogs were ferocious as well as noisy and dirty, and Mr Watson was distraught with the nuisance he had to endure.

The board empathized with Mr Watson's dilemma and ordered that Mr Pother be given notice that the nuisance had to stop. If it did not, he would be dealt with according to the law.

Looters

During the Second World War, looting was a serious problem in Dover. The looters stripped bombed houses bare, removing living-room and stair carpets, beds, entire suites of furniture, and mangles. It was described by Chief Inspector Perry Datlen of Dover CID on 17 April 1942 as '… the greatest organized looting that has yet taken place.' This despicable crime caused severe financial hardship for the victims who had already seen their family homes laid waste.

The houses of Princes Street, now boarded up.

Blackout

When war broke out, a new crime was created, that of negligence in the very serious duty of ensuring all blackout precautions were taken. This may seem a small crime, but there was no room for excuses – one mistake could mean the loss of many lives. On the 8 and 9 July 1939, there was a practice run involving fifteen counties, including Kent, in a test blackout. People in Dover were instructed to cover their windows, while cars drove only on sidelights. Beacons and traffic lights had sacks or hoods draped over them. As a result of the exercise, the chief warden in Rolvenden, Kent was informed that his post had been bombed and that he was badly injured. Strapped to a stretcher, he was rushed off to casualty, an inspired publicity stunt which must have been a talking point over many a dinner table.

The proper blackout began on the 1 September 1939, when Poland was invaded. Sirens (Moaning Minnies) began sounding soon after Neville Chamberlain's wireless announcement at 11.00 a.m. on Sunday, 3 September that England was at war. Soon people were appearing in police courts charged with failing to follow the blackout regulations. A florist in Dover appeared in court for having a light in his top window. He spent some time explaining that he had carefully blacked out all his windows but accidentally knocked on an electric switch with his elbow. The judge was not impressed, and the florist was fined ten shillings.

XVI

THE DOVER AND FOLKESTONE MUTINIES OF THE FIRST WORLD WAR

Some crimes of past times seem to us today not to be crimes at all, not least that of the mutiny of the troops during and after the terrible carnage of the First World War. Nor were mutinies confined to Britain. German, Italian, French and Russian soldiers were shot in large numbers as a result of refusing to fight or walking off the battlefields; sixty British soldiers were shot for cowardice and desertion during 1916. A year later the number was 221, and in 1918, there were 676 executions. After 40,000 French troops had withdrawn from fighting in 1917, the British Army bore the brunt of the war, so it is hardly surprising the figures escalated as they did as the war drew to a close.

Once the Armistice was declared in November 1918, the soldiers naturally wanted to get home to their loved ones as quickly as possible. At his election, with the intention of courting votes, Lloyd George had promised them exactly that, but the military had other ideas. There was talk of men being sent to fight the Bolsheviks in Russia, and although it was promised that only volunteers would be enlisted, common knowledge indicated that men had been conscripted unwillingly.

A soldier in Shoreham, enraged by the treatment of one of his comrades by an officer, walked out, and it took the efforts of a general to calm the men down. The soldiers stood their ground and, next day, 1,000 men were demobilized. A few weeks later, there were disturbances at Dover and Folkestone. The Folkestone soldiers had many grievances against the harsh discipline of their officers, as well as poor living conditions in the camp and the fear of being sent off to fight again. Then came the harsh news that Folkestone soldiers were to be sent back to France. The men announced that, until their demands were taken seriously, no military vessels would be permitted to leave from Folkestone for France, and they followed this up by planting pickets around the harbour. Men arriving back from the battlefields of France joined the demonstrators in their protest.

The men were surprisingly patient. Without undue force, they managed to repel fusiliers armed with bayonets and ball cartridges sent to discipline them. On Saturday a procession of around 10,000 men set off to march through Folkestone and received the support of the people. The soldiers formed a union with officials of their own and soon, Sir William Robertson arrived from the War Office to hear their demands. He allowed the men to elect demobilisation committees from their own numbers.

Georgian barrack houses at Dover Castle dating from the 1740s (in Georgian times, soldiers had to sleep two to a bed!).

Meanwhile, 4,000 Dover soldiers, equally disillusioned with the futility of their situation and harsh conditions at camp, stood firm in support of the soldiers of Folkestone. The Dover men held a meeting at harbour station to form a deputation, and they too decided to march in procession, presenting themselves at the town hall to confront the mayor. It is recorded that they were entertained with some welcoming piano music and invited to attend a film at a nearby Dover cinema.

The politician Horatio Bottomley, MP and editor of *John Bull*, was known as 'the soldiers' friend', and he helped to calm the situation. Ministry of Labour officials speeded up the paperwork so the men could be demobilised. The Dover and Folkestone soldiers became role models for a number of other troops and the War Office was beside itself with the protests. Before too long, many other desperate soldiers were discharged and allowed home to their families.

XVII

A MOTIVE FOR MURDER

On 3 January 1941, the *Dover Express* reported a charge of attempted murder against Charles Arthur Tilbury, aged nineteen, of No. 10 Coombe Close, Dover. His victim was a fair-haired girl of sixteen-and-a-half, Primrose Edwards, who worked as an usherette at the Royal Hippodrome, Dover, and the incident, which could so easily have proven fatal, took place on Saturday 7 December the previous year.

Tilbury, an unemployed merchant seaman of above-average intelligence and with a talent for writing, was defended by Mr J.H. Mowll. The prosecutor was Mr J.F. Claxton. Charles Tilbury's talent was an item in the evidence against him, since when he was arrested, a short story with rather sinister undertones was discovered in his pocket.

The story began: 'He was a quiet inoffensive young fellow who, even in his schooldays, seemed to be burdened with troubles one usually comes into contact with in later years.' The story described how the story's character, Charlie, became one of the rough, bad lads of the area to avoid looking like a 'pansy' among his associates. His parents were dead, and he'd turned to petty stealing. By the age of eighteen, Charlie was put on probation and, eventually, sent to borstal among the 'scrapings of the East End gutter.'

The fictional Charlie was born under the sign of Cancer, the crab, and although he could be a good friend, he was prone to murderous rages when thwarted. On meeting a young girl, Charlie fell in love at first sight, but when she rejected him some time later, he almost committed 'the first murder Dover had known for years', but curbed the instinct to retaliate. Eventually, he met another girl and the two of them become close, even looking forward to setting up their first home together. When war broke out, a steward from a destroyer in Dover Harbour, described as 'tall and smirky', wrecked everything for Charlie. The story-book Charlie tried everything to get his girl back, including reason, entreaties, threats and blackmail. He tried, without success, 'to forget her and then a cold anger overtook him.'

The real life Charles Tilbury met Primrose Edwards of No. 8 Saxon Street, Dover in June 1939. In the summer of the same year, Primrose Edwards and Charles Tilbury had been out and when he returned her to her home at 11.20 p.m., she told him she could not see him any more, as she had 'got into trouble.' Tilbury was distraught and refused to leave her alone. On Thursday, 5 December, when Primrose was working as an usherette at the Royal Hippodrome, Tilbury went to see her, to tell her he had come to say goodbye. He had received calling-up papers for the Merchant Navy, but first he wanted to ask her to return to him. Primrose repeated she did not wish to see him any more.

On Saturday 7 December, Primrose saw Charles Tilbury in the gallery of the Hippodrome at 6.00 p.m. and the two of them spoke together. At 7.30 p.m., her new boyfriend, Mr Douglas

Dover at dusk. The harbour sometimes brought unwelcome visitors like the 'tall and smirky' steward of Tilbury's story.

James Heyman, arrived on the scene. Douglas Heyman was twenty-one years old and a labourer, and he lived at No.141 Folkestone Road. The two young people had known each other for about ten weeks.

Primrose left them alone while she went to collect her pay from downstairs. Meanwhile, Charles Tilbury asked Douglas Heyman to speak to Primrose on his behalf, and, rather surprisingly, the other young man agreed. However, Primrose was still uninterested in her ex-boyfriend. When she returned to the gallery, she put her chocolate tray on the floor and sat down on a back bench.

Both young men were standing behind her, Tilbury a little to the left and, as the lights dimmed, Primrose cried out as she felt a sharp blow in her back. Tilbury had plunged a knife into her left shoulder. Heyman heard the scuffle, and saw Tilbury pulling the knife out and attempting to stab her again. Primrose cried, 'He has stabbed me in the back.' Mr Heyman tried to grab Tilbury, but he escaped and fled, pursued by some soldiers. Primrose collapsed into Douglas' arms.

PC Metcalfe of the war reserve was on duty in Snargate Street at the time, and at 9.00 p.m. was called to the Royal Hippodrome. Primrose was still sitting on the floor and needed first aid to stem the flow of bleeding. The injured girl was taken to Dover Casualty Hospital at 9.40 p.m. and, according to Dr W.G. Sutcliffe, the acting medical superintendent: 'She had two wounds in her back, one behind the right shoulder near the joint and the other behind the left blade bone.' According to the doctor, the right wound was the most severe as the knife narrowly missed cutting an artery and could easily have been fatal.

Meanwhile, Charles Tilbury had run to PC Hodgson at the Prince of Wales Pier. 'I have stabbed a girl at the Hippodrome,' he yelled. PC Hodgson quickly relieved him of his knife.

Another policeman, PC Langley, helped arrest Tilbury, who asked how Primrose was and insisted he didn't intend to do it but she kept ignoring him. Then his story, *Motive for Murder,* was found in the pocket of his bloodstained raincoat; he told the officers that he had written it in the library that morning, but he kept insisting he hadn't meant to kill her at all – only to scare her. Primrose was in hospital for four to five days.

Primrose's mother, Rose, said that Tilbury had expressed a wish to marry her daughter on her birthday, which was on the 20 July, but Rose felt Primrose was far too young and banished Tilbury from the house. Tilbury told her that if he saw Primrose with any other man he would 'do them both in.' The case presented a dilemma for the magistrates, who discussed the necessity of deciding whether he had intended to kill Primrose or to teach her a lesson. It was decided Tilbury should be tried at Maidstone for attempted murder.

At his trial on 28 February 1941, Tilbury was described as, 'one of the best boys who had passed through an approved school'. A medical report claimed that there was nothing wrong with Tilbury, but that there had been: 'a rather terrible history of insanity in the family.' Detective Inspector Datlen explained that Tilbury's mother had died when he was two years old and that he was raised by his grandparents in Dover. At fifteen he was sent to an approved school for housebreaking, (from January 1935 to January 1938) and he had been employed on ships until March 1940. On his return to Dover he worked for Government contractors and his trade was that of an electrician. Tilbury claimed he had once opened a shop in Dover with another young man, although it was bombed and he was rendered unconscious.

The charge of attempted murder was dropped for that of grievous bodily harm, and Tilbury was sentenced to nine months' imprisonment.

XVIII
ARISE MY LOVE!

On Friday 11 July 1941, the *Dover Express* reported a 'Brutal Attack with an Axe.' The victim was George Thomas Roberts, manager of the Plaza Cinema in the Metropole Buildings at No. 20 Cannon Street, Dover. His gruesome murder, committed on the night of 3 July 1941, provoked both anger and disbelief. George Roberts had only been in his post for four months, having previously worked as assistant manager at the Regent Theatre in Gillingham. The *Dover Express* said: 'The first intimation that all was not well was when Mr Roberts failed to turn up at the bank at the usual time on Friday to pay in the previous day's takings.'

A heavily-built man, aged fifty and about five feet eight inches tall, George Roberts, who lived in Second Avenue, Gillingham, was in the habit of sleeping in his office overnight on a mattress he kept rolled up while not in use. When the night watchman, Sidney Williams, aged forty-four, who doubled as a cleaner, began his round after the programme finished at 9.30 p.m., there was no reason for concern that George Roberts was not around. Sidney Williams merely assumed George was tired and was having a nap, so he left at 8.00 a.m. the following morning, unaware that anything was wrong. However, as George Roberts' boss Mr Sidney Sale said later at the inquest, 'We saw things that looked funny.'

At 8.00 a.m. the women cleaners had arrived to spruce up the vestibule, staff room and offices. In the staff room a young cleaner, Mrs Rhoda Foot, aged eighteen, noticed that a framed photograph and a vase had been moved from the window sill onto a shelf. She also had an extra duty to perform – there was a strange dark stain on the tiled floor. Naturally, she scrubbed it away. Another cleaner, Mrs Hannah Southwell, aged forty-two, found more stains on the carpet in George's office, but she decided he'd been ill and treated the stains with disinfectant. Some towels seemed to be missing, but everything else was in order. The mattress was rolled up with George's pyjamas and dressing gown neatly folded on top. Then a third cleaner, Mrs Bertha Roberts, thirty-nine, who was not a relative of the victim, discovered the keys of the safe lying on the floor, but again, she suspected nothing. At the time, the cleaners were all working independently and did not discuss the 'funny things' later described by Sidney Sale.

When George's secretary Ellen Tolputt arrived at the cinema, she put the keys in the safe to find the float had vanished. She became suspicious and immediately telephoned Sidney Sale, the senior manager in Dover for Associated British Cinemas, owners of the Granada and the Plaza. Mr Sale agreed to send an assistant to the Plaza and when the assistant checked the money in the safe, there was £32 unaccounted for. Learning of the theft, Mr Sale arrived in due course and it was thought that George Roberts had absconded with the cash. There was no option but to call the local CID.

The Metropole building once housed the Plaza Cinema.

Detective Inspector Datlen and Detective Constable Thain were told that George had gone to the Friends Social Club in the evening, and Ellen Tolputt said she last saw him around 10.30 p.m. The detectives examined the stains, and then started searching for further evidence. In the basement, they found a stain on the cement floor which looked as though someone had tried to remove it. In a recess at the far end, Sidney Sale discovered the horrible murder. George's head had been split open, and there were three gashes on the right side of his head.

It was time for reinforcements. Scotland Yard sent along Chief Inspector William Rawlings and Detective Sergeant Marshall. It was puzzling – there was no sign of a forced entry, and no fingerprints could be found, so it seemed the murderer was familiar with the premises and was presumed to be a local man. (Yet, according to another newspaper report, several exits and entrances to the cinema remained open during the hours of darkness to facilitate fire-watching duties!) Finally, a horrible discovery was made in the basement: a bloodstained hatchet of the type often used for firefighting.

Sir Bernard Spilsbury came to Dover to visit the crime scene, and he also performed the grisly post-mortem. At the inquest on Wednesday 9 July, he reported three wounds to the front of the head on the right side, close together, two of which had penetrated completely through the skull and which were two and a half, and one and a quarter, inches long. The fourth wound was on the left of the back of the head and was one and a quarter inches long. Death was due to multiple fractures of the skull and injury to the brain. The hatchet was sent for examination to Hendon Laboratories, along with the bloodstained clothing.

By the time of the inquest, there had been so much in the London papers that the coroner felt compelled to warn the jury that they must forget what they had seen and go entirely on the evidence. Then he said, 'It is one of the worst cases I have heard in my forty years' experience as a coroner … I have not had anything quite so brutal and vicious.' Evidence was given identifying the murdered man and it was established the last person to see George Roberts alive was his secretary. It was claimed he had no known enemies, nor any serious quarrels with anyone, and that he was a person of good character. Then the coroner adjourned the inquest. George Roberts' funeral took place the following day at Charing Crematorium and his ashes were scattered in the Garden of Remembrance.

Interviews with the staff established each had an alibi, so no arrests could be made. The case had drawn nationwide interest, as the previous Saturday, the 5 July, the *News of the World* had sent a special crime reporter to Dover and published a long account the following day. The reporter wrote: 'After interviewing scores of people in Dover, they [the police] are convinced there is someone in the town who unwittingly holds a clue which may lead to the arrest of the slayer.' On the 18 July, the *Dover Express* ran a column with the byline 'Search for Silent Witnesses', stating that the police were convinced robbery was not the motive for the crime, but that Mr Roberts had a secret enemy. The opinion of the journalists was that Dover's first mystery murder would be an unsolved one unless the person who could speak did not 'persist in remaining silent'. But the papers spoke too soon, for the detectives were still working on the case.

Leslie Hammond, an operator at the Plaza, was summoned to appear at the police station. Hammond had been standing outside the cinema with his brother until 9.55 p.m. on the night in question. He'd already given the detectives an account of a long walk he had taken along the local streets on his fire-watching duties. Detective Inspector Rawlings totalled up the time Leslie Hammond's route should have taken and found a discrepancy of between twenty and fifty minutes, depending on whether Hammond had arrived at the Midland Bank at 11.00 p.m. or 11.30 p.m. It was enough to call the youth in for questioning.

Dover police station.

Dover's little River Dour.

On being confronted with the discrepancy in time, Hammond feigned confusion, saying he felt funny because of Mr Robert's death and could not think properly. But he was no match for the sharp detective, and eventually he confessed to the murder. He had arrived at the cinema after 10.00 p.m., and hung around in the vestibule waiting for George Roberts. Earlier that same day, he had hidden the murder weapon in a switch room. George Roberts was hit with the hatchet as soon as he entered the vestibule, and then struck again when he crumpled to the floor.

Hammond described how he had tied a tablecloth around the bleeding man's head and hauled him to the staff room, planning to leave him in the basement. Afraid that the nightwatchman Sidney Williams might witness the act, he couldn't take the corpse through the auditorium, so he threw it out of the window into the basement area, a drop of twelve feet and six inches, then ran downstairs and dragged it into the little room. Despite all this, he kept a clear head and worked on the floor stains with a towel, finally draping George's coat over his body. Cold-bloodedly, he emptied the safe and slung the hatchet out of the window of the female staff room, first removing the photo frame and vase and climbing on the windowsill. Then Hammond said, 'I went to the gents and was sick,' although it is not clear whether this was prompted by squeamishness or remorse.

Hammond returned to his fire-watching duties, hiding the money in the cistern of a public house toilet. Later £18 was discovered in the cistern of the outside toilet at his house and a body search revealed a number of silver coins hidden in his underpants in a Plaza cinema bag. Hammond's trial took place at the Old Bailey on Friday 19 and Monday 22 September 1941 and was reported by the *Dover Express* on Friday, 26 September. Mr G.B. McClure, Mr Curtis Bennett and Mr Maxwell attended for the prosecution and Mr B.H. Waddy and Miss D. Knight Dix defended.

Mr Saunders, foreman at the Plaza, claimed an axe was kept in the rewind room, but that he saw it in the switch room prior to the murder. He felt it must have been put there by a person who intended to use it. Elsie Finney, who was also on fire-watching duty on the night of the murder, said that Hammond had arrived at the Midland Bank 'perspiring very heavily'. His shirt was wringing wet, and he was out of breath and agitated, but he explained away his condition by saying he was late after taking his girl home.

Hammond's confession was read to the court, part of which is as follows:

'I heard Mr Roberts come through the side door. I dodged into the switch room. I picked up the axe that was in there and then went out into the vestibule and hit Mr Roberts with the axe. He fell down and I struck him in the face. I put him on the floor. I hit him again with the axe.'

Defending counsel Mr Waddy requested permission from the judge to dismiss the jury as he had a submission to make. This was that Hammond's mistreatment by the police on 21 July 1941 made the evidence inadmissible. Hammond's allegations, mostly against Detective Sergeant Datlen, were that he had been smacked in the face, called a liar and had his arm twisted behind his back. Other incidents of hair-pulling and ear-twisting were also submitted. The police denied

Modern, Victorian and twelfth-century Dover.

all the charges, and it was stressed that Detective Sergeant Datlen was never alone with the prisoner. The submission by the defence was rejected.

Then Mr Waddy claimed there was a history of epilepsy in Hammond's family. In his summing-up, which took sixty-five minutes, Justice Cassells stated that there was no proven connection between epilepsy and murder and described it as a 'very wicked and cruel crime'. The jury retired for thirty-five minutes and returned to pass the guilty verdict on Leslie Hammond. Mr Justice Cassells put on his black cap to tell Hammond he would be hanged by the neck until he was dead. Hammond appealed, without success, in October. Then the Home Secretary intervened, and, on 11 November 1941, Hammond was reprieved, his sentence commuted to penal servitude.

George Roberts left a widow and a seventeen-year-old son who was a commercial artist. The name of the film showing on that fatal night was *Arise my Love* – a poignant irony.

Afterword

It seems a paradox to suggest that a book about crime and murder might bring a place more to life for the reader. Yet, that is what I hope this book will achieve. Dover's past, valiant and robust as well as dark and sinister, has helped make the town what it is today, a vibrant area steeped in its own fascinating history. The gruelling nature of my research has given me many sleepless nights – even so, I am glad to know Dover a little better and to understand something of the complex social history that made people behave the way they did. In this way, we understand ourselves more fully. These personal stories demonstrate the darkest sides of the human character, but they also offer encouraging glimpses of the resourcefulness and, ultimately, the development of ordinary people that sometimes culminates in acts of great compassion and heroism. If we only look at the 'nice' side of life, then I think we are only half a person, because we are all, deep inside, a mixture of dark and light in varying degrees – like the world we live in, past, present and future.

Bibliography

This Sceptred Isle by Christopher Lee, Penguin Books/BBC Books (1997)
Smuggling in Kent and Sussex, 1700-1840 by Mary Waugh, Countryside Books (1985)
Kent Lore, by Alan Bignell, Robert Hale (1983)
A History of Kent, by F.W. Jessup, Phillimore & Co. Ltd (1995)
A Second Kentish Patchwork, by Robert H. Goodsall, Stedehill Publications (1963)
The Place Names of Kent by Judith Glover, Meresborough Books (1976 and 1982)
Crime and Criminals in Victorian Kent by Adrian Gray, Meresborough Books (1985)
Shipwrecks of the Goodwin Sands, by Richard and Bridget Larn, Meresborough Books (1995)
Murder in Kent, by Philip MacDougall, Robert Hale (1989)
Local Studies resources, Dover, Margate, Westgate and Birchington Libraries.

Other local titles published by The History Press

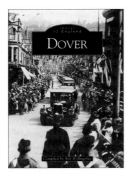

Dover

BOB HOLLINGSBEE

This compilation of over 220 photographs and other illustrations, many of which have never been published before, has been drawn from the author's extensive collection and the archives of the *Dover Express*. It explores the last 150 years of life in this historic port, capturing not only major historic events such as the evacuation from Dunkirk and the visits of dignitaries such as Winston Churchill but also the everyday life of the town and its people.

0 7524 1622 7

Folklore of Kent

FRAN AND GEOFF DOEL

This fascinating book explores the folklore, legends, customs and songs of Kent, and the causative factors underlying them. From saints to smugglers, hop-pickers to hoodeners, mummers to May garlands, wife sales to witchcraft, this book charts the traditional culture of this popular and culturally significant southern county.

0 7524 2628 1

Haunted Kent

JANET CAMERON

Haunted Kent contains spooky stories from around the county, including the hunchbacked monk at Boughton Malherbe, the black dog of Leeds and the well-known tale of Lady Blanche of Rochester Castle. This intriguing collection of strange sightings and happenings in the county's streets, churches, public houses and country lanes is sure to appeal to anyone wanting to know why Kent is known as the most haunted county in England.

0 7524 3605 8

Old Kent Inns

DONALD STUART

Old Kent Inns tells of spy-holes and smugglers, of cock-fighting, ghosts, buried treasure, murders and hangings, of escaped convicts and Siamese twins, phantom ships, hidden tunnels, hiding places and bodies bricked into walls. Discover why Ellen Blean poisoned her master with a meat pie or the inn where Ruth Ellis once dined: with tales of locals villains such as the landlord 'Nasty face', who sold women into slavery from behind his bar for three shillings apiece, and of the notorious Dick Turpin, take a journey through the old inns of Kent.

0 7524 3959 6

If you are interested in purchasing other books published by The History Press, or in case you have difficulty finding any of our books in your local bookshop, you can also place orders directly through our website

www.thehistorypress.co.uk